Warman's
JOHN DEERE
Collectibles

David Doyle

Identification and Price Guide

©2008 David Doyle
Published by

krause publications
An Imprint of F+W Media, Inc.

700 East State Street • Iola, WI 54990-0001
715-445-2214 • 888-457-2873
www.krausebooks.com

Our toll-free number to place an order or obtain
a free catalog is (800) 258-0929.

Library of Congress Control Number: 2008929069
ISBN-13: 978-0-89689-696-3
ISBN-10: 0-89689-696-X

Designed by Kay Sanders and Donna Mummery
Edited by Justin Moen

Printed in China

3 1561 00228 5207

DEDICATION

Dedicated to the American farmer—the only businessperson in the world with no say in what his or her products sell for—yet feeding, clothing, and now fueling, much of the world!

Warman's® Identification and Price Guide series

Warman's® Antiques & Collectibles Price Guide
Warman's® Carnival Glass
Warman's® Children's Books
Warman's® Civil War Collectibles
Warman's® Civil War Weapons
Warman's® Coca-Cola Collectibles®
Warman's® Coins & Paper Money
Warman's® Cookie Jars
Warman's® Costume Jewelry Figurals
Warman's® Depression Glass
Warman's® Dolls: Antique to Modern
Warman's® Duck Decoys
Warman's® English & Continental Pottery & Porcelain
Warman's® Fenton Glass
Warman's® Fiesta Ware
Warman's® Flea Market Price Guide
Warman's® Gas Station Collectibles
Warman's® Hull Pottery
Warman's® Jewelry
Warman's® Little Golden Books
Warman's® Majolica
Warman's® McCoy Pottery
Warman's® North American Indian Artifacts
Warman's® Political Collectibles
Warman's® Red Wing Pottery
Warman's® Rookwood Pottery
Warman's® Roseville Pottery
Warman's® Sporting Collectibles
Warman's® Sterling Silver Flatware
Warman's® Vietnam War Collectibles
Warman's® Vintage Jewelry
Warman's® Weller Pottery
Warman's® World War II Collectibles

Warman's® Companion series

Carnival Glass
Collectible Dolls
Depression Glass
Fenton Glass
Fiesta
Hallmark Keepsake Ornaments
Hot Wheels
McCoy Pottery
PEZ®
Roseville Pottery
U.S. Coins & Currency
Watches
World Coins & Currency

ACKNOWLEDGMENTS

The sheer number of items carrying the John Deere name and logo staggers the imagination. Because this is such a vast area, it would be impossible for a single book to include everything, and likewise it is impossible for a single collection to be all encompassing. A book of this scope would be impossible to create without the eager and willing help of many collectors and enthusiasts.

Particularly helpful during the research and preparation of this book were Dave McEachren, who enthusiastically shared not only a portion of his knowledge, but also his collection of toys, promotional material, and matchbooks. Bob Johnson, whose passion for corn pickers is unmatched, and who provided much of the advertising material about these and other machines. Dale Lenz has a formidable collection of factory and dealer items, as well as early promotional trinkets, and was a great help with these items. Allen Eggers, Jerry Erickson and Justin Moen patiently allowed us to photograph key items from their collections, and answered innumerable questions.

Kris Kandler and Doug Mitchell took many of the outstanding photographs in this book, and these were supplemented by photographs generously provided by Jane Aumann of Aumann Auctions, including images and sales data on some extraordinarily scarce items.

Neil Dahlstrom, archivist, opened the John Deere archives for our research, enhancing the material presented herein.

CONTENTS

INTRODUCTION

John Deere Collectibles, More Than Knick-Knacks—A Legacy

John Deere—the name has had instant recognition for generations. Even to this day grammar school texts mention John Deere's 1837 development of the self-scouring steel plow as one of the keys to the nation's development. John Deere, the company, has been a constant thread throughout generations of farmers.

From that hammering and polishing of his first steel plow in Grand Detour, Ill., until 1868, the blacksmith from Vermont had various partners, and the firm had various names. But in 1868, Deere and Co. was incorporated in Moline, Ill., with John Deere as president, son Charles Deere, nephew George Vinton, and son-in-law Stephen Velie as shareholders. Like so many farms, Deere and Co. was largely a family business. Today, Deere and Co. is still operating, and is the parent company of a worldwide manufacturing concern.

1868!!! That was the year Ulysses S. Grant, hero of the Civil War, won election as President of the United States. Wilbur Wright had not yet had his first birthday, and Orville was yet to be born. The same year, a couple hundred miles east of Moline, the Studebaker brothers opened a wagon works, Henry Ford was five years old, and John Deere had already been making plows for 31 years—and still is!

It is this "constant" of John Deere that is appreciated by collectors, many of which farm. College texts and Wall Street marketing types refer to "agribusinessmen." Indeed, they are businessmen—but walk into a tractor dealership, stop by a co-op, or go into a country store and ask the guy wearing the dirt and sweat-stained green hat what he does, and the answer you get is not "I am an agribusinessman"—its "I farm"—stated with simple pride. It is this unpretentious pride and work ethic that is passed down from generation to generation that connects with Deere and Co. Unlike many of their competitors, who through mergers and the influence of marketing school graduates have seen once proud names as Oliver, Allis-Chalmers, J.I. Case, and International succumb to much more sterile and new names like "Agco" and "Case-IH," Deere and Co. remains Deere and Co.

Such subtle consistency becomes tradition, and tradition is a part of the farming culture. Even today, many a tractor is driven from the "home place" down to the "Johnson place," even though the Johnsons sold out and moved into town in 1957. But that 200 acres was called the Johnson place by granddad, who had dinner with the Johnsons after they helped each other with the threshing, and it will likely always be the Johnson place. A similar tradition and heritage pervades equipment purchases. It is rare to drive past equipment sheds that 10 years ago were filled with green machines and today filled with orange or red, or vise-versa. Sons and grandsons of farmers today are buying their 9030s from the sons and grandsons of the men that sold their forefathers their Model Ds, 720s and 4020s.

Many a farmer imagines their great-grandfather harnessing the mules to a walking plow, and then great-grandpa, Mike and Jake, and John Deere farmed together. Or his grandfather, protected by a simple umbrella, listening to the distinctive melodic popping exhaust as he and John Deere—this time a new Model A—labored under the blazing hot sun. Today, climbing into the air-conditioned cab of his 8030 to work the same ground, he appreciates the hard labor his ancestors did, alongside their best farm hand, John Deere.

It is this tradition that brings about the nostalgia associated with the items in this book. For many, decorating the office of the family farm with these collectibles is a way to connect with the past, a tribute to their ancestors, a memorial to the sweat and hard work they did to create the family farm—the farm with which they are now entrusted. For others, the items in this book represent a simpler time in life—rarely "the good ol' days"—for farming has always been hard work, but a time when the world seemed slower, and few problems couldn't be fixed with the help of a neighbor.

Like many, I entered the world of John Deere through my father. Though my mom was the daughter of a farmer, and was born and raised on the farm, we never farmed. For most of my childhood my father ran a fertilizer business in a small town, so farmers and farm life was no stranger to me. When I was in my teens, my dad changed jobs, and began managing a John Deere dealership. I spent my share of time cleaning up the shop, delivering parts, and standing behind the parts counter, leafing through heavy green and black binders looking for obscure part numbers—and passing out those "farm management notebooks" as the pocket ledgers came to be known.

The dealership changed hands and, of course, this meant a new array of promotional materials had to be bought. Matchbooks, pens, atlases, and host of other items were discarded—replaced with new items with the new name. How I now wish I'd been a bit more of a pack rat then.

Eventually, like many of my contemporaries, I went off to college—where in my dorm room I ate frozen pizza off paper plates printed with "John Deere" around the outside, and wiped my face with napkins similarly marked. Dad left the implement business, and except for a 1977-78 John Deere Rand-McNally road atlas that was my constant traveling companion for years, Deere and I drifted apart…until a chance encounter with some collectors brought a series of "I remember these" and "I remember when…." remarks from me.

Some collectors specialize in paraphernalia related to their family farm, gathering the brochures and manuals for the equipment that worked the home place. For others, the primary emphasis of their collection is the equipment itself, with operator's and service manuals, as well as sales material being merely an adjunct to their core collection. Some collect items by series, for example, seeking an example of each year's Pocket Ledger, or every toy John Deere made by Ertl.

Whether a novice or veteran collector, my key advice is to buy what you like, at a price you are comfortable with. Resist the temptation to buy something just because it is a "good deal"—if you don't really like the item—how good of a deal can it possibly be?

Beware too of increasing numbers of counterfeit and forgery items. When in doubt, ask a more experienced collector, and remember the old adage—if it sounds too good to be true, it probably is!

CHAPTER 1
SELLING DEERE—
ADVERTISING
LITERATURE

Yesterday, as today, sales brochures and advertising literature were most often the first contact that farmers had with new Deere products. The leadership at Deere has recognized the conditions of the American farmer, and these catalogs are expertly tailored to them. The brochures were frequently colorful, in order to be eye-catching, and practical. Typically working from well before sunrise until nightfall, the farmer did not have time to waste reading a lot of "fluff"—nor would they have much patience for firms sending out the same. This is not to mention the reaction to a company not delivering on its advertising.

Yesterday's sales brochures have become today's collectibles, and interest in this area is increasing. Tractor collectors not surprisingly covet the brochures applicable to their equipment, while others gather the brochures relating to equipment once found on the family farm. Still, other collectors simply try to gather an example of each type of tractor, corn picker, combine or other implement.

John Deere has produced a variety of periodicals through the years, ranging from the monthly *Furrow*, to the annual *Better Farming* and *Modern Farming*. Articles in these magazines provide valuable tips and insight into more efficient, and profitable, crop production, and of course the magazines are liberally sprinkled with John Deere advertising.

The colorful printing that once appealed to potential customers finds favor with collectors, and the configuration of these brochures and catalogs make them easy to store relatively compactly in filing cabinets and binders.

The familiar "pocket ledger"—created to be an aid to farm accounting—plus, of course a frequent reminder of the dealer whose name appeared on the front cover. While many collectors today prefer mint, unsoiled examples, the soiled, used examples full of notations provide interesting insight into life on the farm for generations gone by, and are collectible in their own right.

Colorful calendars have been issued through the years. The artwork on these featuring everything from today's Deere implements at work to elaborate paintings of rural life or landscapes (often featuring a deer) in years gone by.

Most of these items were intended to have a short life—to pique interest in an item, bring the farmer into the showroom, and help the dealer make the sale. Unlike owners and service manuals, they were not intended to become a permanent part of a library. Hence, the binding was inexpensive, as was the paper stock. Indeed, by far the majority of these items were discarded long ago—which is precisely what makes them collectible today.

Sales Brochures — Tractors

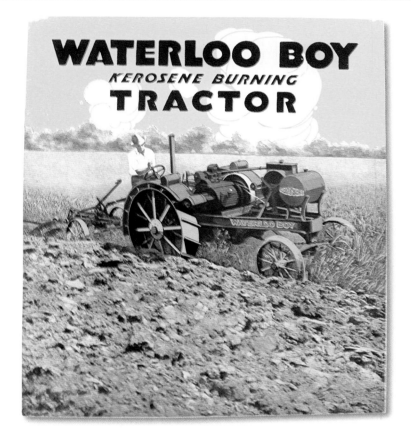

A 28-page Waterloo Boy catalog. **$375-425**

Very early 10-page Waterloo Boy catalog with yellow cover. **$225-275**

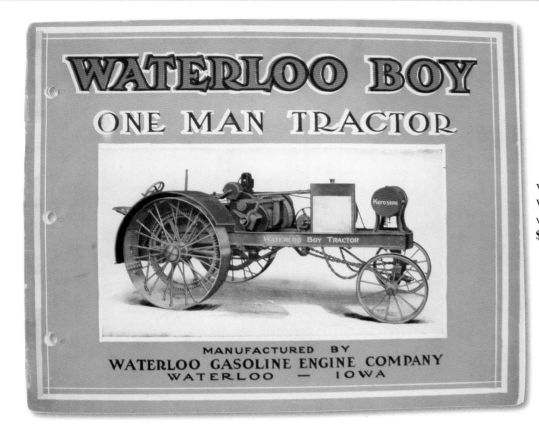

Very early 26-page Waterloo Boy catalog with gray cover. **$500-600**

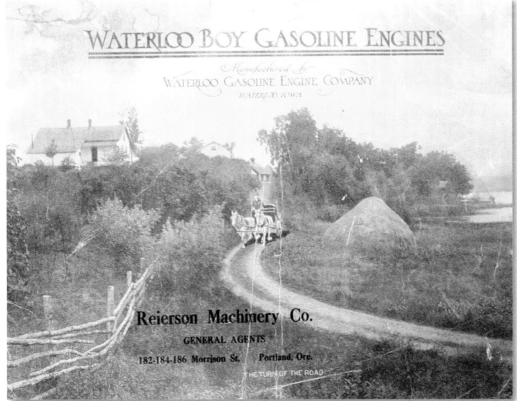

Circa 1910-11 Waterloo Boy catalog. **$225-275**

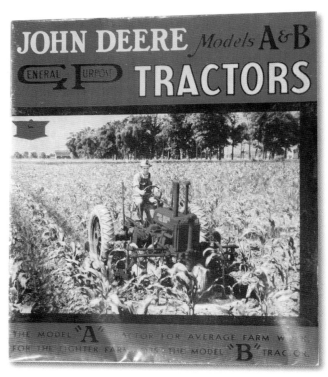

John Deere A & B sales booklet, 1936 issue. **$100-125**

Sales literature for the Model N Overtime tractor. English version of the Waterloo Boy. **$200-250**

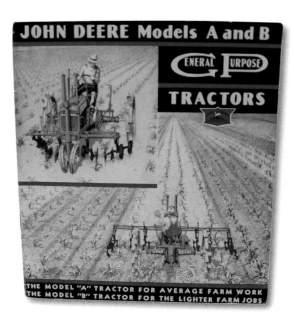

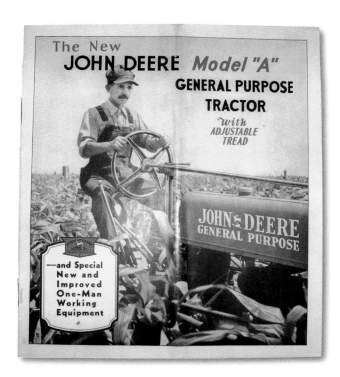

Early issue John Deere sales booklet for Model A. **$225-275**

John Deere A & B sales booklet, 1935 issue. **$225-275**

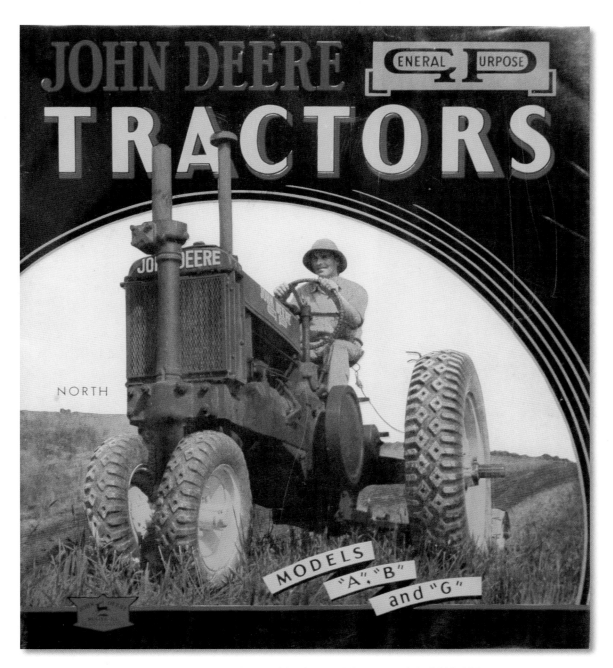

1938 John Deere sales booklet for Models A, B and G. **$100-125**

1928 John Deere sales booklet for Model D. **$80-100**

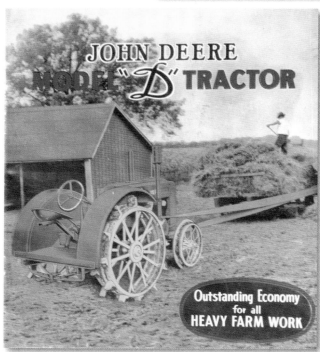

1940 John Deere sales booklet for Model D. **$80-90**

John Deere sales booklet for Model H. **$100-150**

John Deere sales
booklet for Model H.
$100-150

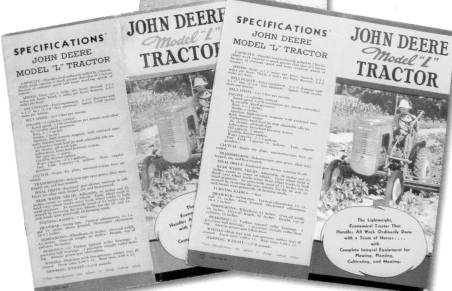

Two different styles
of John Deere styled
L sales booklets.
$65-85 each

Two different styles of John Deere Model M sales booklets. **$65-85 each**

John Deere Model M sales booklet. **$40-60**

Two different styles of John Deere Model MT sales booklets. **$100-125 each**

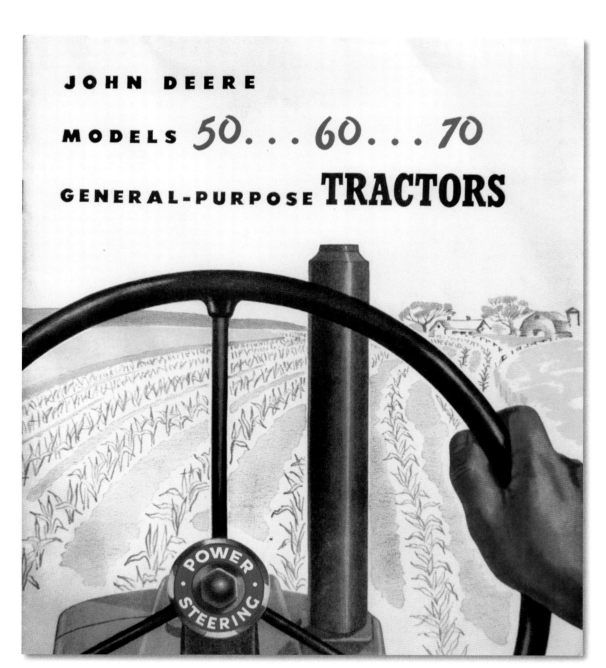

1954 sales booklet of 50, 60 and 70 series tractors. **$40-50**

1964 110 Lawn and Garden tractor sales booklet. **$60-80**

Sales booklet for 430 crawler tractor. **$100-125**

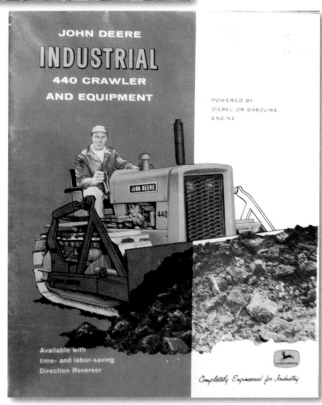

1959 sales booklet for 440 crawler tractor. **$50-60**

1973 sales booklet on 820 tractor and skid-steer loaders. **$8-15**

1960 sales booklet for 1010 tractor. **$20-30**

1966 sales booklet for 1020 and 2020 tractors. **$15-20**

Sales booklet for 3010 and 4010 tractors. **$40-50**

Yesterday's sales brochures have become today's collectibles, and interest in this area is increasing.

1966 sales booklet for 3020 and 4020 tractors. **$40-50**

Sales booklet for 5010 tractor. **$40-50**

1968 sales booklet on 2520, 3020 and 4020 row-crop tractors. **$40-50**

1968 4520 tractor sales booklet. **$30-40**

Sales booklet for 5020 diesel tractor. **$40-50**

1918 John Deere sales brochure on binders. **$150-250**

Two different John Deere Beet and Bean Equipment sales booklets. **$65-85 each**

1969 John Deere sales booklet on Bedders and Listers. **$8-15**

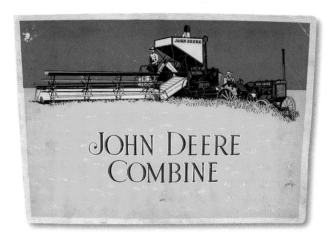

John Deere 24-page booklet on the No. 1 and No. 2 combines. **$125-225**

Early John Deere sales booklet on Binders, Mowers and Rakes. **$300-350**

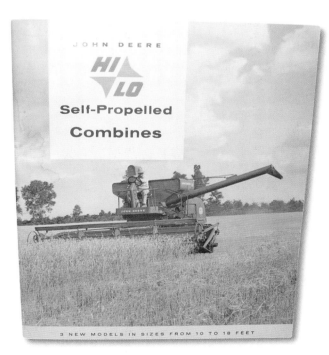

1960 John Deere Hi-Lo self-propelled combines sales booklet. **$30-40**

1938 sales brochure on No. 10 one-row corn picker. **$10-20**

1939 sales brochure on No. 15 two-row corn picker. **$10-20**

1931 sales brochure on No. 20 two-row corn picker. **$10-20**

1955 sales brochure on 127 one-row corn picker. **$10-20**

1946 sales brochure on 226 two-row corn picker. **$10-20**

1959 sales brochure on 227 two-row corn picker. **$10-20**

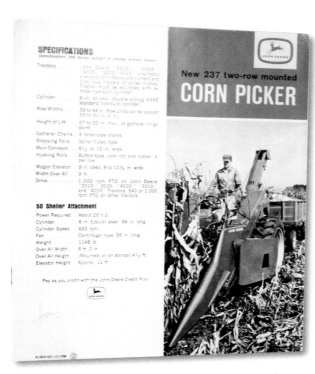

1963 sales brochure on 237 two-row corn picker. **$10-20**

1969 sales booklet on Row-Crop Cultivating Equipment. **$8-15**

1971 sales booklet on Row-Crop Cultivating Equipment. **$8-15**

1965 sales booklet on Disk Tillers and Rod Weeders. **$8-15**

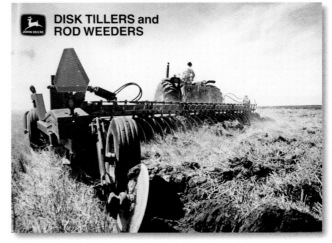

1969 sales booklet on Disk Tillers and Rod Weeders. **$8-15**

1969 sales booklet on Drawn and Integral Disk Harrows. **$8-15**

1960s sales booklet on Earth Shaping and Irrigation Equipment. **$8-15**

1971 sales booklet on Drawn and Integral Disk Harrows. **$8-15**

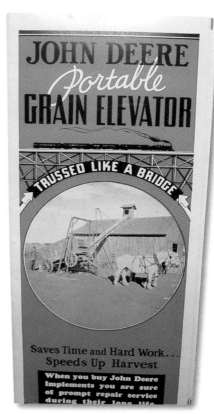

Sales brochure on John Deere portable grain elevators. **$10-15**

1960s sales booklet on Earth Shaping and Irrigation Equipment. **$8-15**

1955 sales brochure on 18-1/2-inch bale-size elevators. **$8-12**

1976 sales booklet on Feeding, Material Handling, and Special-Use Equipment. **$8-15**

1977 sales booklet on Feeding, Material Handling, and Special-Use Equipment. **$8-15**

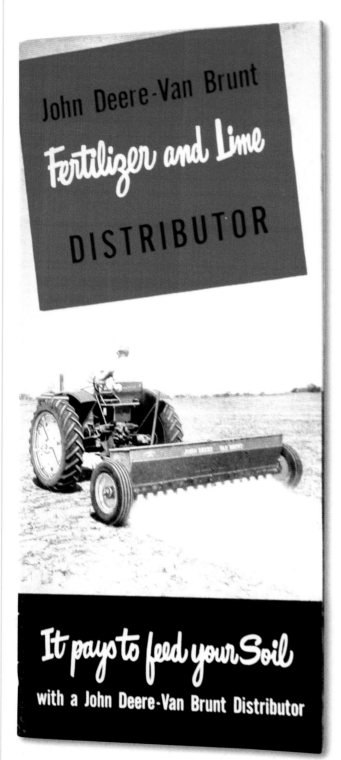

1946 sales brochure on John Deere – Van Brunt Fertilizer and Lime Distributor. **$8-12**

1950 sales brochure on John Deere – Van Brunt Fertilizer and Lime Distributor. **$8-12**

1964 sales brochure on John Deere Fertilizer Distributor. **$8-12**

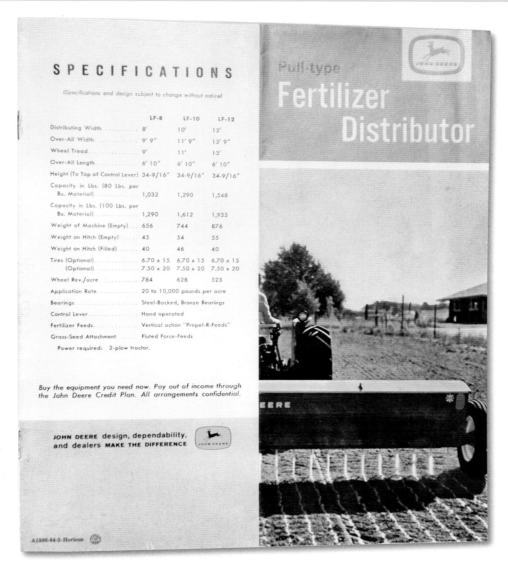

SPECIFICATIONS

(Specifications and design subject to change without notice)

	LF-8	LF-10	LF-12
Distributing Width	8'	10'	12'
Over-All Width	9' 9"	11' 9"	13' 9"
Wheel Tread	9'	11'	13'
Over-All Length	6' 10"	6' 10"	6' 10"
Height (To Top of Control Lever)	34-9/16"	34-9/16"	34-9/16"
Capacity in Lbs. (80 Lbs. per Bu. Material)	1,032	1,290	1,548
Capacity in Lbs. (100 Lbs. per Bu. Material)	1,290	1,612	1,935
Weight of Machine (Empty)	656	744	876
Weight on Hitch (Empty)	45	54	55
Weight on Hitch (Filled)	40	46	40
Tires (Optional)	6.70 x 15	6.70 x 15	6.70 x 15
(Optional)	7.50 x 20	7.50 x 20	7.50 x 20
Wheel Rev./acre	784	628	523
Application Rate	20 to 10,000 pounds per acre		
Bearings	Steel-Backed, Bronze Bearings		
Control Lever	Hand operated		
Fertilizer Feeds	Vertical action "Propel-R-Feeds"		
Grass-Seed Attachment	Fluted Force-Feeds		
Power required:	2-plow tractor.		

Buy the equipment you need now. Pay out of income through the John Deere Credit Plan. All arrangements confidential.

JOHN DEERE design, dependability, and dealers MAKE THE DIFFERENCE

Pull-type Fertilizer Distributor

A1886-64-2-Horicon

1971 John Deere sales booklet on Field Finishing Equipment. **$8-15**

1972 John Deere sales booklet on Field Finishing Equipment. **$8-15**

1964 John Deere sales pamphlet on Forage Harvester. **$8-15**

1972 John Deere sales booklet on End-Wheel and Press Grain Drills. **$8-15**

1969 John Deere sales booklet on Hi-Cycles and Sprayers. **$8-15**

1969 John Deere sales booklet on End-Wheel and Press Grain Drills. **$8-15**

1971 John Deere sales booklet on Sprayers and Hi-Cycles. **$8-15**

1973 John Deere sales booklet on Sprayers and Hi-Cycles. **$8-15**

1960s John Deere sales booklet on Sprayers and Hi-Cycles. **$8-15**

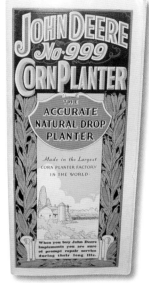

John Deere 999 Corn Planter brochure. **$40-50**

1971 John Deere sales booklet on Rotary Cutters and Flail Shredder. **$8-15**

1969 John Deere sales booklet on Rotary Cutters. **$8-15**

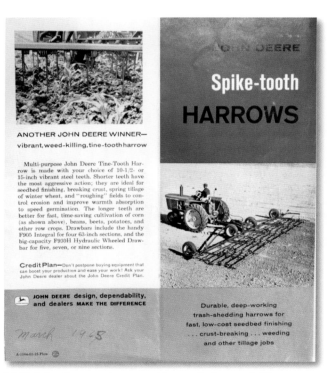

1961 John Deere sales pamphlet on Spike-tooth Harrows. **$8-15**

1971 John Deere sales booklet on Rotary Cutters and Flail Shredder. **$8-15**

1941 John Deere sales pamphlet on Manure Handling Equipment. **$8-15**

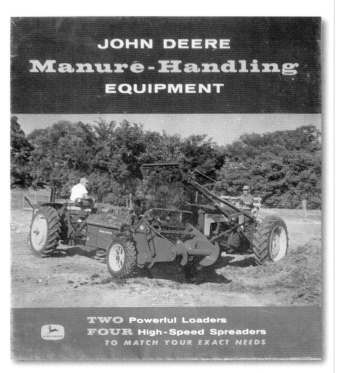

1959 John Deere sales booklet on Manure Handling Equipment. **$20-25**

1969 John Deere sales booklet on Manure Handling Equipment. **$8-15**

1971 John Deere sales booklet on Manure Handling Equipment. **$8-15**

1969 John Deere sales booklet on Materials Handling and Feeding Equipment. **$8-15**

1972 John Deere sales booklet on Materials-Handling and Feeding Equipment. **$8-15**

John Deere sales booklet on 494, 495, 694 and 695 Corn Planters. **$20-25**

John Deere sales booklet on 494-A and 495-A Corn Planters. **$8-12**

1964 John Deere sales booklet on four-, six- and eight-row Corn Planters. **$10-15**

1954 John Deere sales pamphlet on Potato Planters. **$15-20**

1969 John Deere sales booklet on Unit Planters. **$15-20**

1969 John Deere sales booklet on Drawn and Integral Chisel Plows. **$8-15**

1971 John Deere sales booklet on Drawn and Integral Chisel Plows. **$8-15**

1972 John Deere sales booklet on Drawn and Mounted Chisel Plows. **$8-15**

1967 John Deere sales booklet on Moldboard Plows. **$15-20**

1969 John Deere sales booklet on Moldboard and Disk Plows. **$15-20**

1971 John Deere sales booklet on Moldboard and Disk Plows. **$8-15**

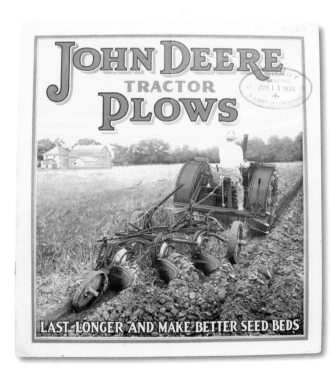

John Deere Tractor Plows sales booklet. **$200-250**

1962 John Deere sales pamphlet on rakes. **$8-15**

1978 sales booklet on Skid Steer Loaders. **$8-15**

1969 sales booklet for Tool Carriers and Toolbars. **$8-15**

1958 sales booklet for 530, 630 and 730 Matched Working Equipment. **$20-30**

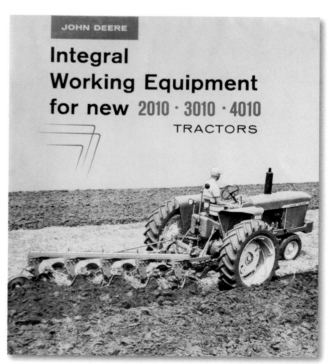

1960 sales booklet for 2010, 3010 and 4010 Matched Working Equipment. **$20-30**

Better Farming, Modern Farming and Other Promotional Literature

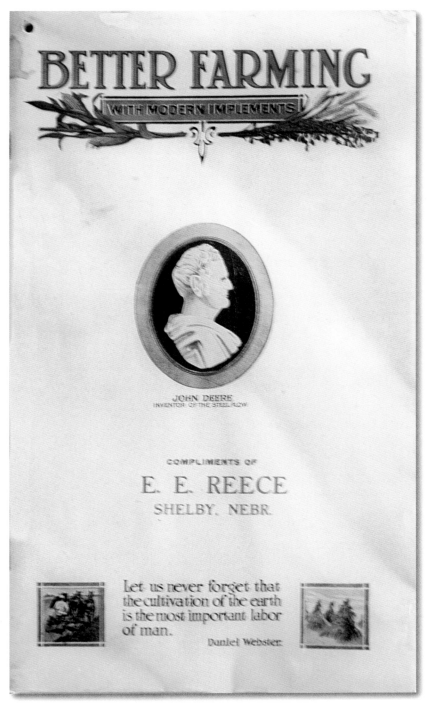

Early 78-page *John Deere Better Farming* annual magazine produced by John Deere extensively featuring Deere equipment. **$150-200**

Better Farming for 1935, 104-page edition of an annual magazine produced by John Deere extensively featuring Deere equipment. **$50-200**

Better Farming for 1940, 1940 edition of an annual magazine produced by John Deere extensively featuring Deere equipment. **$75-100**

Better Farming for 1942, 1942 edition of an annual magazine produced by John Deere extensively featuring Deere equipment. **$75-100**

Better Farming for 1945, 1945 edition of an annual magazine produced by John Deere extensively featuring Deere equipment. **$75-100**

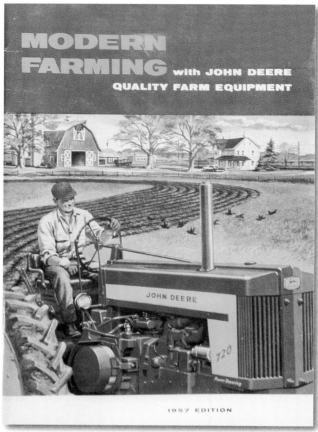

1955 issue of *Modern Farming*, successor John Deere annual magazine to *Better Farming*. **$40-60**

1957 issue of *Modern Farming*, successor John Deere annual magazine to *Better Farming*. **$50-75**

1961 issue of *Modern Farming*, successor John Deere annual magazine to *Better Farming*. **$50-75**

1965 issue of *Modern Farming*, successor John Deere annual magazine to *Better Farming*. **$25-50**

The Furrow Magazine. John Deere began publishing this magazine in 1895—and continues to do so today! **$5-50**

The Furrow Magazine, spring 1913. **$30-50**

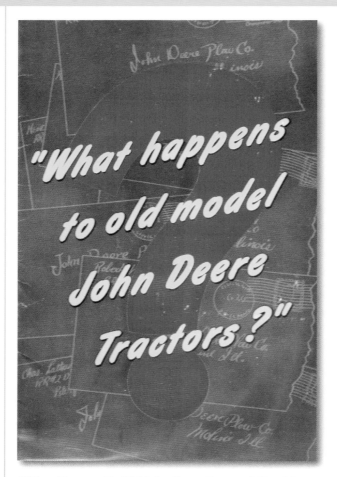

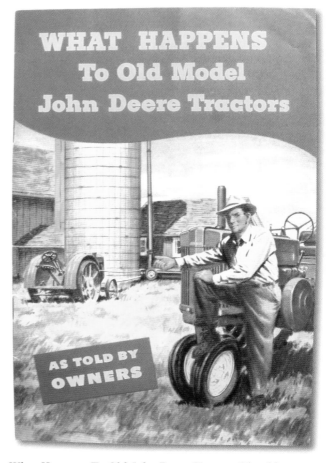

"What Happens To Old John Deere Tractors?" booklet, early version. Book is used to show that older tractors continue to be used for light-duty work on the farm. **$50-75**

What Happens To Old John Deere Tractors? booklet, 1954 edition. **$25-50**

Facts from the Factory, John Deere promotional literature emphasizing preventative maintenance, 1945. **$25-50**

In the mid-20th century, John Deere produced a number of small promotional pieces designed to be mailed to dealer's customers, or potential customers. **$5-50 each**

Even postcards and envelopes were used as promotional items during the first part of the 20th century, and today some are quite collectible. **$10-75 each**

1934 Power Farming, John Deere promotional material for the entire line of tractors and farm equipment. **$100-125**

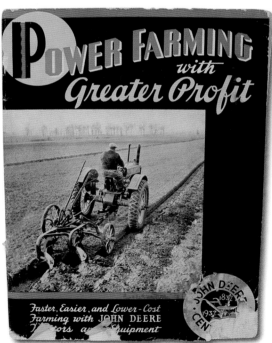
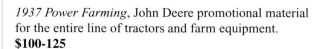

1937 Power Farming, John Deere promotional material for the entire line of tractors and farm equipment. **$100-125**

More and Better Corn, 1918 issue, 24 pages. **$300-350**

John Deere Better Crops at Lower Costs. **$75-100**

"Greater Earning Power on the Farm - John Deere Quality Implements," 164-page booklet. **$120-150**

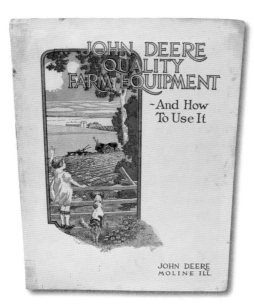

"John Deere Quality Farm Equipment and How to Use it," early 160-page book. **$140-200**

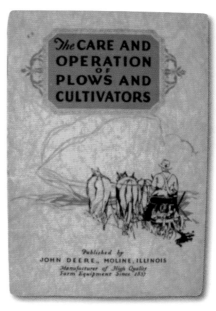

John Deere 64-page booklet on "Care and Operation of Plows and Cultivators." **$25-50**

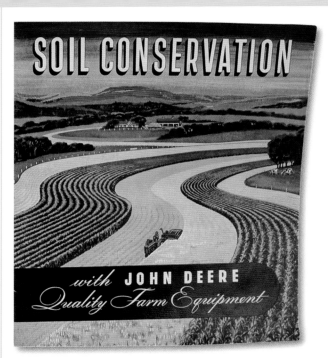

John Deere 32-page "Soil Conservation" booklet. **$25-40**

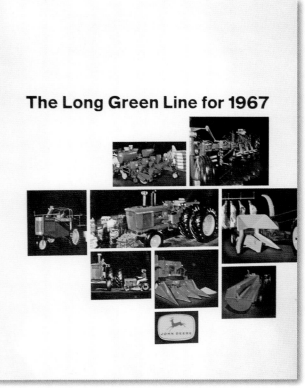

"The Long Green Line for 1967," 96 pages. **$20-25**

The Long Green Line Gets Longer, 1972 pamphlet. **$25-35**

What's New for '71 from John Deere, 1971 pamphlet.
$25-35

Moline Wagon Co. advertising postcard. **$40-60**

John Deere card,
showing sulky
plow. **$20-40**

John Deere
card with kitten
illustration,
promoting plows
and cultivators.
$40-60

Deere & Mansur Co. card. **$175-225**

Deere & Mansur Co. cattle card. **$70-100**

Deere & Mansur Co. ram sheep card. **$80-120**

Deere & Mansur Co. dog card. **$80-110**

John Deere Colonial baler twine postcard. **$75-150**

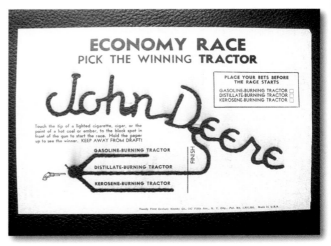

Card, designed to be set on fire, promoting John Deere's superior fuel economy. **$100-200**

John Deere Fertilizer postcard. **$200-300**

1886 Deere & Co. calendar. **$3,000-4,000**

1890 John Deere chromolithograph calendar. **$3,000-4,000**

1896 Deere & Co. calendar. **$2,000-3,000**

1906 John Deere Dallas Branch House calendar with embossed stag. **$400-500**

1908 Deere calendar with embossed John Deere bust. **$600-700**

1915 Deere calendar with embossed John Deere bust. **$300-400**

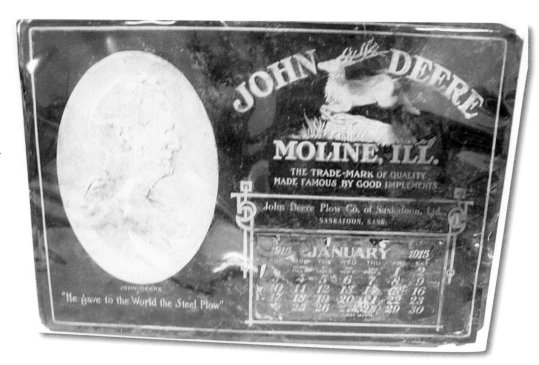

1926 John Deere calendar. **$100-150**

1927 John Deere calendar showing John Deere walking plow. **$400-500**

1928 John Deere calendar with stag scene. **$150-250**

1928 John Deere calendar with woman. **$200-300**

1929 John Deere calendar with un-styled D tractor. **$400-500**

1930 John Deere calendar with un-styled D tractor. **$400-500**

1931 John Deere calendar with un-styled D tractor. **$400-500**

1932 John Deere calendar with un-styled D tractor. **$400-500**

1933 John Deere calendar with un-styled D tractor. **$800-1,000**

1934 John Deere calendar with un-styled D tractor and binder. **$800-1,000**

1937 John Deere Centennial calendar. **$500-600**

1939 small format John Deere calendar with styled A.
$150-200

1938 calendar with un-styled A. **$300-400**

1939 large format John Deere calendar with styled A.
$225-275

1940 John Deere calendar showing wagon, A and combine. **$100-125**

1941 John Deere calendar with lake scene. **$50-75**

1940 large format John Deere calendar showing wagon, A and combine. **$225-275**

1941 John Deere calendar with tractor disking field. **$150-200**

1942 small format John Deere calendar with B and cultivators. **$75-125**

1943 John Deere calendar with Model B pulling manure spreader. **$225-275**

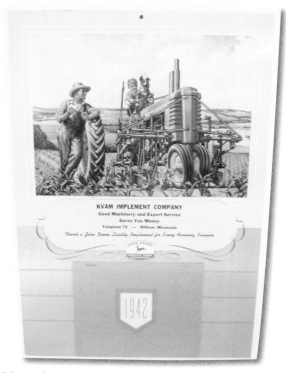

1942 large format John Deere calendar with B and cultivators. **$225-275**

1944 John Deere calendar with boy and girl in front of dealership. **$400-450**

1945 John Deere calendar with styled G and convoy of army 6 x 6 trucks. **$250-300**

1946 John Deere calendar with Model B pulling wagon.
$250-300

1947 John Deere calendar with boy driving Model A.
$250-300

1948 Canadian John Deere calendar with real photo.
$150-175

1948 U.S. John Deere calendar with painting of same scene as shown in Canadian photo. **$200-250**

1950 John Deere calendar with styled A. **$800-1,000**

1954 John Deere American Bird Book calendar. **$60-75**

1951 John Deere calendar with Model B pulling wagon.
$275-325

1975 John Deere kitchen style calendar. **$10-20**

Pocket Ledgers

1878 Pocket Companion. **$175-250**

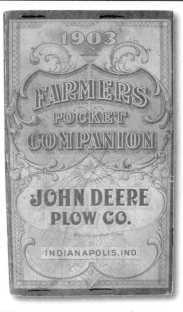

1903 Pocket Companion. **$175-250**

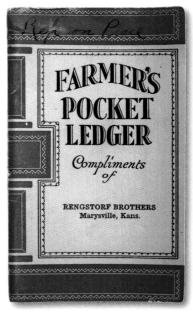

1928, 62nd edition Pocket Ledger.
$50-75

1878 Pocket Companion. **$175-250**

1921, 55th edition of the Pocket
Ledger. **$175-225**

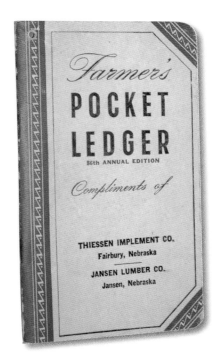

1952, 86th edition Pocket Ledger.
$15-20

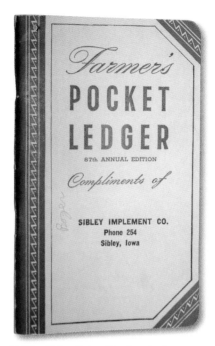

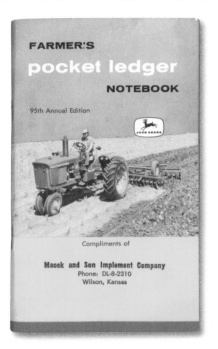

1953, 87th edition Pocket Ledger. **$10-15**

1961, 95th edition Pocket Ledger. **$10-15**

1962, 96th edition Pocket Ledger. **$10-15**

Later editions of the Pocket Ledger (also known as the Farm Management Notebook) featured a variety of cover illustrations. **$5-15 each**

CHAPTER 2
ALWAYS AT HAND—
ADVERTISING
TRINKETS

Subtler than the direct marketing brochures discussed in the previous chapter, most of the advertising trinkets emblazoned with the John Deere name or logo are of utilitarian nature. Pens, pencils and lighters are all items that would be reached for frequently—and hopefully the frequent exposure to the brand and dealer name would reinforce their relationship with their customer.

Rain gauges, thermometer and weather vanes all provide information to the farmer that is beyond handy. Such information may be casually interesting to someone in town, but for the farmer, weather conditions can dictate not just the day's work, but the year's success. Hence, these items are referred to daily.

Tape measures and knives are found in the pockets of most farmers, so where better to put

the familiar green and yellow colors with the famed deer logo? Farming is not a job; it's a way of life, for everyone in the family. Equipment has always been expensive—for most Americans their largest purchase is their home—not so for the farmer. Tractors, combines and cotton pickers all cost many-fold the price of a home. The decision on making such an investment is not taken lightly and rarely without the support of the farmer's partner—his wife. So it is not surprising that Deere included ladies in their marketing efforts, from the pretty, feminine calendars in the previous chapter to colorful (and today, very collectible) mirrors listed in this chapter.

The singular exceptions to the utilitarian nature of the items in this chapter are the advertising buttons. They've been included in this chapter simply by default, as they certainly are advertising, but aren't literature. Buttons such as these were very popular during the first half of the 20th century, promoting everything from political candidates to candy bars, and it's not surprising that a number of buttons were made featuring various John Deere products and branch houses. In more recent times the popularity of producing such items seems to have diminished, perhaps replaced by self-adhesive stickers and silk-screened shirts. However, for the collector, interest in the buttons of by-gone years has never been higher.

Large celluloid pin-back button with bust of John Deere and legend "Inventor of the Steel Plow John Deere." **$50-80**

Celluloid John Deere Waterloo Boy button. **$400-600**

Early gold and cobalt blue enamel buttonhole button advertising Deere & Co., Moline, Ill. **$250-350**

Large green celluloid pin-back button with bust of John Deere and legend "John Deere He Gave to the World the Steel Plow." This was produced in conjunction with the Deere centennial. **$50-80**

Large celluloid buttonhole button advertising Deere bicycles that reads: "If you love me grin!" **$600-750**

Celluloid buttonhole button advertising Deere bicycles. **$400-600**

Celluloid buttonhole button advertising Deere bicycles. **$400-600**

Large celluloid buttonhole button with brass trim advertising "Up-to-Date" saddles, harnesses and collars offered by the John Deere Plow Co., Kansas City, Mo. **$2,750-3,250**

Pin-back celluloid button one inch in diameter advertising "White Elephant" brand saddlery and vehicles. White elephant items were sold through Deere's catalogs in the 19th century. **$400-500**

Pin-back celluloid button one inch in diameter advertising "Up-to-Date" saddles and harnesses offered by the John Deere Plow Co. **$750-850**

Mansur & Tebbets Implement Co., St. Louis "White Elephant" buttonhole button. **$500-600**

Pin-back button from John Deere Plow Co. of Omaha, Neb., advertising Columbus Buggys. **$400-500**

Pin-back celluloid button one inch in diameter advertising the Velie Saddlery Co., Kansas City, Mo. **$1,000-1,200**

Cobalt blue and white Velie Automobile button. **$350-450**

Celluloid pin-back button advertising Velie, with "The Name Insures the Quality" legend. **$200-250**

John Deere Bettendorf wagon pin, Davenport, Iowa. **$40-80**

Seven-eighths-inch diameter celluloid pin-back button advertising "John Deere Power Steering." **$25-35**

Pin-back "chirper" button from John Deere Button Omaha Branch, John Deere Plow Co. **$750-1,000**

John Deere 6600 side hill combine flicker button. **$80-100**

Early red John Deere Plow Co., Kansas City, Mo., buttonhole button. **$750-1,000**

John Deere flicker button with four-legged deer. **$80-100**

Ashtrays

"Success" Manure Spreader tip or ashtray. **$100-200**

Square glass ashtray with John Deere Quality Farm Equipment logo. **$50-70**

John Deere Quality Farm Equipment logo plastic ashtray. **$70-80**

John Deere Lanz pottery ashtray. **$80-100**

John Deere Lanz ashtray.
$200-250

Glass ashtray with John
Deere Quality Farm
Equipment logo from
Alefs & Sons, Great Bend,
Kan. **$60-80**

Letter Openers

All-brass letter opener, "Velie" on one side, "John Deere" on the other side. **$250-300**

Letter opener with Quality Farm Equipment logo on Mother of Pearl handle and folding knife blade. **$200-225**

Letter opener with four-legged deer logo on Mother of Pearl handle and folding knife blade. **$150-200**

Letter opener with four-legged deer logo on green handle. **$75-100**

Letter opener with yellow and green handle, advertising Lynn Implement Co. **$50-60**

Silver-plated letter opener with bust of John Deere on one side, other side has sulky plow. Canadian branch house item. **$500-600**

Centennial letter opener with centennial coin on both sides. **$300-400**

Lighters

Lighter with enamel rendering of dealership, tractors and cotton picker. **$225-275**

Early John Deere Tractor Co. Waterloo bullet lighter, red. **$150-175**

Early John Deere Tractor Co. Waterloo bullet lighter, green. **$125-150**

Argentinean lighter with four-legged deer logo. **$175-200**

South American John Deere lighter with industrial logo. **$125-150**

Lighter with Quality Farm Equipment logo. **$80-100**

John Deere Colonial baler-twine lighter with enamel logo. **$350-450**

Enameled "Sparks New Earning Power" lighter. **$125-175**

Dealer lighter with Quality Farm Equipment logo. **$75-125**

Dealer lighter with Quality Farm Equipment logo. **$200-250**

Lighter with 440 crawler image on the inside. **$175-200**

Lighter with four-legged deer and John Deere Quality Fertilizer logo. **$450-500**

Metal dealer lighter with four-legged deer logo. **$75-125**

Moline Malleable Iron lighter. **$125-175**

Metal dealer lighter with four-legged deer logo. **$75-125**

Metal lighter with four-legged deer logo. **$75-125**

Matchsafes

Matchsafe Sharples Cream Separator. **$900-1,000**

Matchsafe, from John Deere Plow Co., silver-plated, legend on back reads "I believe in the superiority of John Deere goods." **$1,000-1,200**

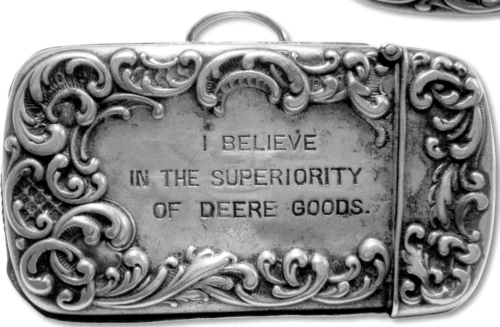

Matchsafe, from John Deere Plow Co., silver-plated, legend on back reads "Manufacturers and jobbers of implements, vehicles, saddlery, wagons, etc." **$1,300-1,500**

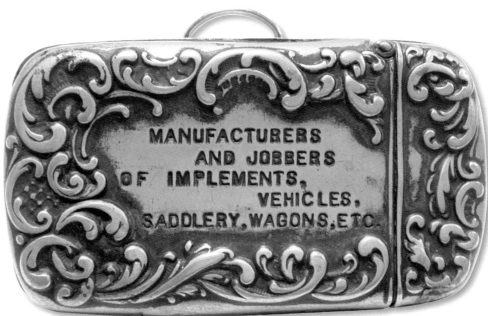

Celluloid matchsafe from
Indianapolis branch with "The
Worlds Standard." logo on back.
$2,900-3,100

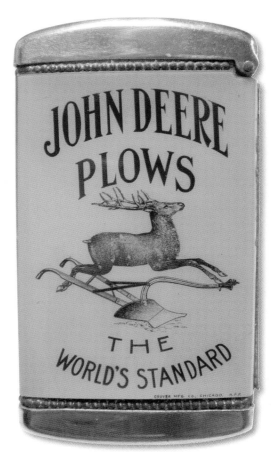

Celluloid matchsafe from Deere and Co. - Moline with woman on front and "The World's Standard" logo on back. **$2,900-3,100**

Celluloid matchsafe from Deere and Mansur Co. **$800-1,500**

Matchbooks

Matchbook with John Deere tractor tear away matches, yellow cover. **$50-75**

Matchbook with John Deere tractor tear away matches, black cover, 1938. **$50-100**

Matchbook with cover featuring John Deere 820 tractor. **$50-75**

Two matchbooks, one early with walking plow, the other a John Deere Industrial matchbook. **$50 each**

John Deere Fertilizer Vitrea Deere logo matchbook. **$75-125**

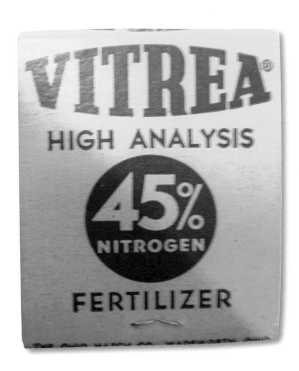

John Deere 45 Fertilizer matchbook. **$75-125**

These matchbooks carry the 1936-1950 John Deere Shield logo, and are imprinted with corporate rather than dealer information. **$25-75 each**

These white matchbooks carry the 1950 to 1956 Quality Farm Equipment logo on one face, and a tractor on the other. The two at left are imprinted with corporate markings, while the two at right have dealer markings. **$25-75 each**

These dealership matchbooks also carry the Quality Farm Equipment logo, but lack the tractor image. The blue matchbook is a bit unusual as compared to the standard green, yellow or white. **$25-75 each**

These green matchbook covers are imprinted with the 1956-1968 four-legged deer logo, and in most cases, dealership information. **$20-40**

Matchbooks, like any other Deere item, marked for Deere's short-lived fertilizer marketing, are especially coveted. **$75-125**

John Deere Industrial dealers also distributed promotional matchbooks. The examples shown here carry the 1968-1999 logo. **$15-35**

Lawn and Garden dealers also use matchbooks as promotional aids. **$15-35**

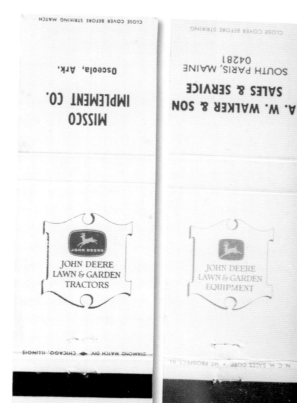

Mirrors and Brushes

Celluloid-backed pocket mirror with emblems of the 10 John Deere companies surrounding deer. **$1,750-3,000**

Celluloid-backed pocket mirror with bust of John Deere. **$700-900**

Celluloid-backed round brush with bust of John Deere. **$500-800**

Celluloid-backed oblong brush with Shield logo. **$500-800**

Oval compact mirror advertising John Deere/Ohio Silo Filler. **$75-125**

Penknives and Sharpening Stones

Early knife advertising John Deere Machinery on one side and Ford cars on the other. **$200-250**

Very early Plow Co. pocketknife with bust of John Deere. Both sides are very ornate. **$700-800**

Two-blade pocketknife, Dakin Implement, with Shield logo on Mother of Pearl grips. **$150-175**

Combination penknife and money clip with Mother of Pearl and four-legged deer in center. **$150-200**

Two-blade pocketknife, Calvin Implement, with Shield logo on Mother of Pearl grips. **$150-175**

Pocketknife with two-legged deer logo. **$40-60**

Pocketknife with Quality Farm Equipment logo. **$100-125**

Pocketknife with four-legged deer logo. **$100-125**

Pocketknife with shield logo and Mother of Pearl grips. **$125-150**

Pocketknife with John Deere Fertilizer, four-legged deer logo on Mother of Pearl grips. **$275-325**

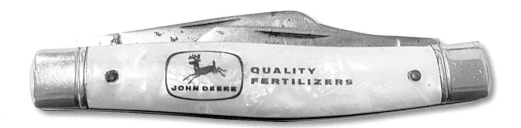

German John Deere Lanz pocketknife, all brass. **$125-175**

German John Deere Lanz pocketknife, brass with green logo, furnished with leather case. **$425-475**

John Deere Manhiem Works knife with leather case. **$125-150**

John Deere centennial sharpening stone with celluloid back, decorated with bust of John Deere. **$500-700**

Pens and Pencils

John Deere 45 Fertilizer matching notebook and bullet pencil. **$100-125**

Pencil with Mother of Pearl inlay and four-legged John Deere industrial deer logo. **$125-150**

Pencil with Mother of Pearl inlay advertising John Deere 350 dozer. **$125-150**

Pencil with Mother of Pearl inlay advertising John Deere 5010 scraper. **$125-150**

John Deere Fertilizer bullet ink pen. **$80-100**

John Deere Plow Co. – Kansas City – Denver, celluloid bullet pencil or needle case. **$350-400**

Pencil with Mother of Pearl inlay advertising John Deere haying equipment. **$65-85**

Pair of pencils, one with Quality Farm Equipment logo, the other with four-legged deer. **$50-75**

Pencil with Mother of Pearl inlay advertising "Intro of Powershift" with New Generation Tractor image. **$125-150**

Early pencil with Mother of Pearl inlay with an H tractor on it. **$125-150**

John Deere pen with Styled A/G from Corwith, Iowa dealer. **$30-50**

Early John Deere pen from Rolfe, Iowa dealer. **$30-50**

Pair of pencils, one with Mother of Pearl inlay and Quality Farm Equipment logo, the other with just the Quality Farm Equipment logo. **$50-75**

Two John Deere dealership bullet pencils. **$15-25**

Pencil topper with Quality Farm Equipment logo. **$20-25**

Rain Gauges, Thermometers and Weather Vanes

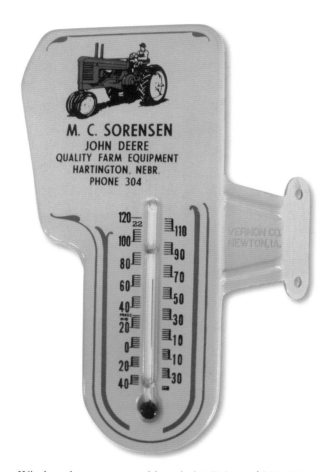

Window thermometer with styled A/B logo. **$350-500**

Knop & McDowell John Deere dealership thermometer on frame picture. **$175-225**

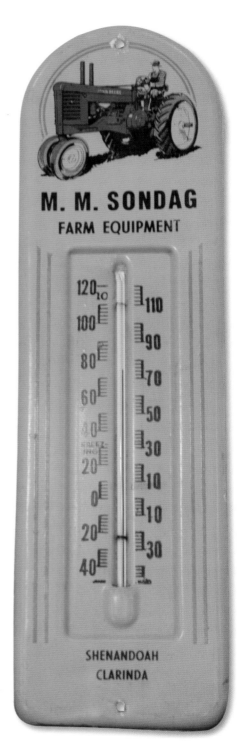

Metal thermometer with styled A/B logo. **$80-100**

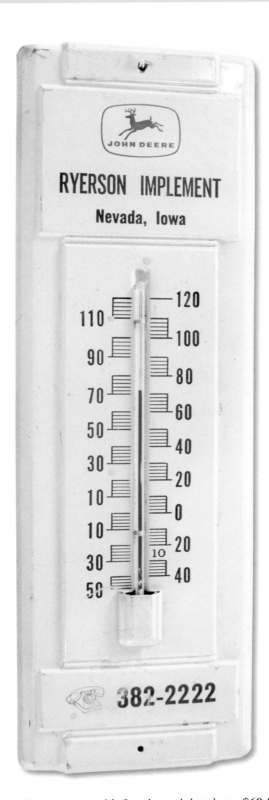

"Keep me you'll never be broke" Alefs & Sons John Deere dealership thermometer. **$60-80**

Metal thermometer with four-legged deer logo. **$60-80**

Combination thermometer, barometer, and rain gauge with styled A/B logo. **$1,000-1,200**

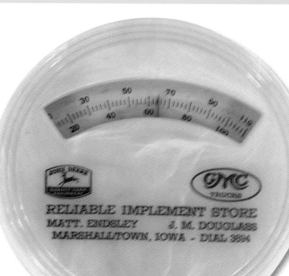

Thermometer with Quality Farm Equipment and GMC logos. **$75-100**

White rain gauge promoting John Deere Fertilizer, with four-legged deer logo. **$200-300**

 Rain gauges, thermometers and weather vanes all provide information to the farmer that is beyond handy.

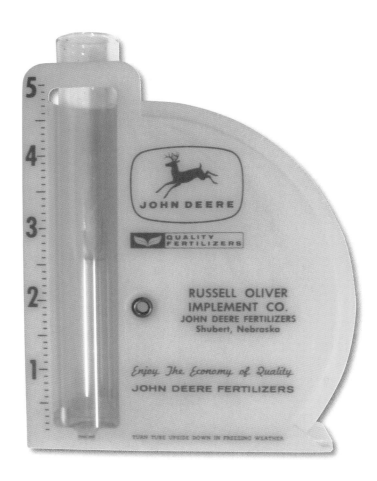

Yellow rain gauge promoting John Deere Fertilizer, with four-legged deer logo. **$200-300**

John Deere Employees Credit Union, Waterloo, Iowa rain gauge. **$40-60**

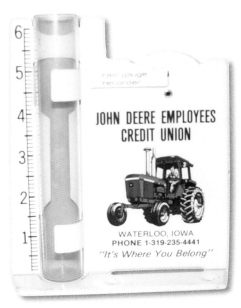

Miniature weather vane with A/B tractor decoration. **$300-400**

Argentinean John Deere weather vane in original packaging. **$200-250**

Tape Measures

Tape measure advertising the John Deere Plow Co., White Elephant Vehicles made of aluminum. **$750-850**

John Deere Plow Co. aluminum tape measure, 1902. **$550-650**

John Deere Plow Co. – St. Louis, aluminum tape measure given away at the 1904 World's Fair in St. Louis. **$750-850**

John Deere Plow Co., Omaha branch, reverse side
reads "John Deere vehicles are All Right." **$1,400-1,600**

Celluloid
tape
measure
advertising John
Deere tubular cream separators.
$550-650

Tape measure advertising Favorite Stoves and
Ranges on one side, other side advertises John
Deere implements. **$250-300**

John Deere Plow Co. celluloid tape measure with three-legged deer jumping over log. Reverse decorated with a bust of John Deere with the legend "He gave to the world the steel plow." **$80-100**

Celluloid tape measure with Quality Farm Equipment logo, reverse decorated with a bust of John Deere with the legend "He gave to the world the steel plow." **$60-80**

Celluloid tape measure with four-legged deer logo. **$60-80**

Plastic tape measure with four-legged deer logo and dealership advertisement. **$60-80**

Square tape measure advertising Gautier Implement Co. **$25-35**

Celluloid tape measure with Quality Farm Equipment logo and dealer imprint. **$150-200**

Post-1968 round metal and plastic tape measure with two-legged deer logo. **$15-25**

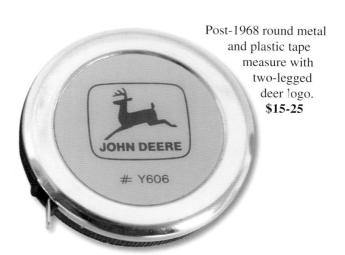

Round tape measure advertising Rule Grain Co., with post-1956 four-legged deer logo. **$25-35**

Green plastic tape measure with four-legged deer logo and dealership advertisement. **$60-80**

Round tape measure with advertisement promoting Hartman Bros. Implement Co. – John Deere dealers. **$25-35**

Metal bank produced during centennial that is designed to look like an oil can. **$150-225**

Waterloo Boys Tractor and Gas Engine, six-inch ruler. **$200-250**

1884 Presidential election bowties. Customers were to enter their guess as to the winner, fold, and mail in. A drawing would then determine which entrant won a new John Deere corn planter. **$600-800**

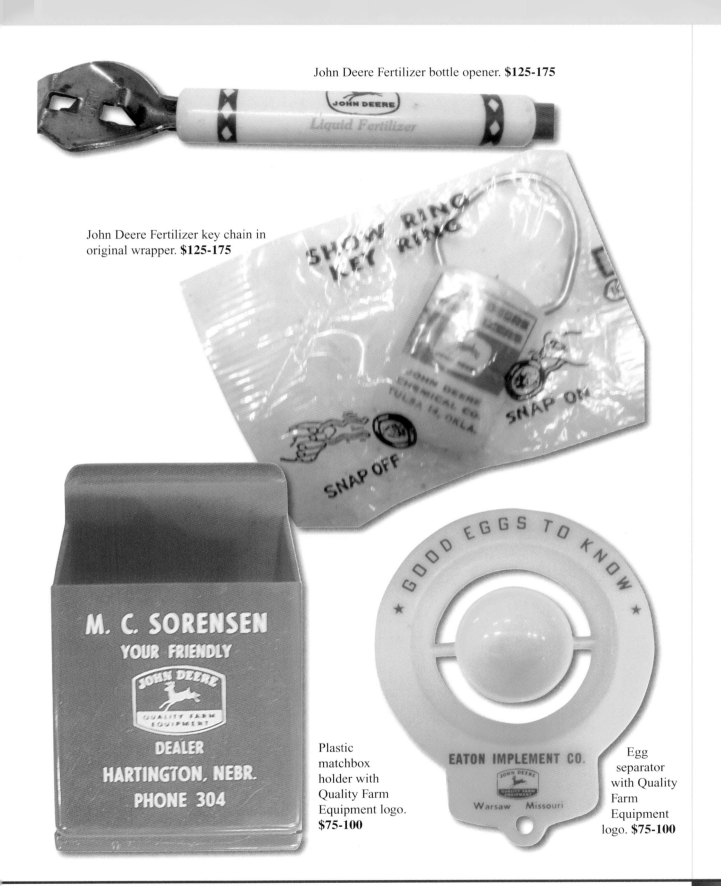

John Deere Fertilizer bottle opener. **$125-175**

John Deere Fertilizer key chain in original wrapper. **$125-175**

SHOW RING KEY RING

SNAP ON

SNAP OFF

JOHN DEERE CHEMICAL CO. TULSA 14, OKLA.

GOOD EGGS TO KNOW

M. C. SORENSEN
YOUR FRIENDLY
JOHN DEERE
QUALITY FARM EQUIPMENT
DEALER
HARTINGTON, NEBR.
PHONE 304

Plastic matchbox holder with Quality Farm Equipment logo. **$75-100**

EATON IMPLEMENT CO.
JOHN DEERE
QUALITY FARM EQUIPMENT
Warsaw   Missouri

Egg separator with Quality Farm Equipment logo. **$75-100**

Double shaker with styled A. **$50-75**

Yellow double shaker with 20 series John Deere tractor. **$75-100**

Green double shakers with the Quality Farm Equipment logo were made in two sizes. **$40-50 each**

Playing cards from John Deere Tractor Co., Waterloo, Iowa with styled A. **$150-200**

Yo-yo with Quality Farm Equipment logo. **$75-100**

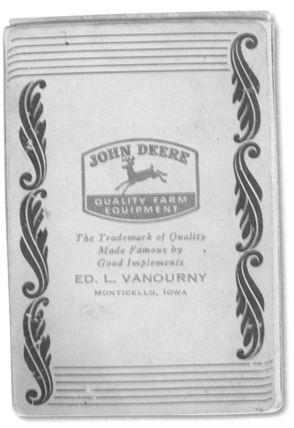

Dealership playing cards with Quality Farm Equipment logo. **$75-125**

Dealership playing cards with 1968 through 1999 logo. **$25-50**

John Deere paperweights, with pictures on bottoms. **$50-75 each**

"Maltese Cross" paper advertising premium. **$175-225**

Thermos with 1968 through 1999 leaping deer logo and "Run with the Best" legend. **$20-30**

Early shield logo license plate topper advertising combination John Deere and Chevrolet dealership. **$225-275**

Mirror decorated with styled A tractor pulling plow. **$225-275**

Set of six drinking glasses with John Deere 20 series tractor on them. **$250-350**

Paper drinking cups, typically found in dealerships of the period. **$3-10 each**

Brass knob walking stick with two-legged John Deere logo. **$40-60**

John Deere drinking glasses with tractors dealer display. **$150-175**

John Deere "Dawn of a New Era Dubuque, Iowa," doorstop. **$40-50**

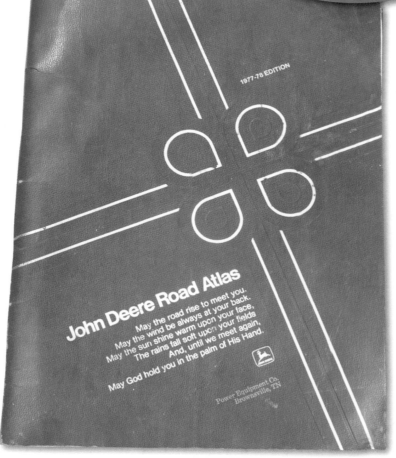

John Deere 4 Rand-McNally U.S. Road Atlas from 1977-78. **$40-60**

White ceramic coffee mug, one side decorated with a Model D, the other bearing the legend "Go With the Green, Go, John Deere Service." **$8-15**

Plastic John Deere nightlight with logo, packaged in black cardboard box, late 1970s. **$5-15**

Set of "Country Heritage" placemats, which feature scenes from the large mural at Deere's worldwide headquarters. Produced in the late 1970s. **$15-35**

CHAPTER 3
WEARING GREEN— CLOTHING AND OTHER APPAREL

Clothing featuring the John Deere name seems to have its origins with dealer and company employee apparel. Oftentimes these were simple work clothes, sometimes supplied by a uniform service, with a John Deere logo patch sewn on, and embroidered dealer and personnel names. Promotional headwear and novelty ties were soon added to the mix. The hats and caps in particular very popular, especially before enclosed all-weather cabs on tractors became commonplace. They were popular too with the dealers and Deere because the hat provided a prominent, and public, place to display the Deere logo. Because the hats were usually used as intended, that is, worn in dusty (or rainy) fields 12 or more hours per day, today pristine examples can be hard to find.

Watch fobs were long popular premiums—at least until pocket watches were no longer commonplace.

Although not as prominent place to position the Deere logo, the fobs were public, and were an item that the customer would see and use on a daily basis.

When Deere began producing snowmobiles, and later, other recreational equipment, a new line of apparel appeared. Rather than targeting employees, these items were to be sold (or in some cases, given) to the consumer. By the late 1970s Deere and Co. marketed a wide range of clothing including shirts, jackets and gloves. Some were given away by dealers to preferred customers, but were assigned "TY" part numbers and provided through Deere's normal parts distribution system, it was clear these goods were intended to be sold. This appears to have been the beginning of an onslaught of goods aimed at a consumer market far beyond those who'd ever climbed on a tractor.

Clothing

Vintage John Deere yellow necktie with tractors. **$50-75**

Vintage John Deere string tie with tractors. **$50-75**

John Deere green underwear. **$50-125**

Brown and gray John Deere neckties. **$15-20 each**

Green nylon jacket from early 1980s. **$25-40**

John Deere fall jacket promoting 10-series combine. **$25-50**

Cast metal belt buckle of 8440 four-wheel drive tractor. **$20-35**

John Deere has marketed many types of gloves through the years, both insulated and leather work gloves, like these. **$10-15 each**

John Deere offered these polo shirts during their 150th anniversary. **$10-20 each**

During the time Deere produced snowmobiles, they also offered snowmobile suits, such as this one. **$100-150**

Hats

Green straw pith helmet with Quality Farm Equipment logo with yellow background. **$225-275**

Hard white pith helmet with four-legged deer logo. **$50-100**

Shop hat decorated with dealership name and Quality Farm Equipment logo. **$150-200**

Green straw pith helmet with Quality Farm Equipment logo with green background. **$125-175**

Straw cowboy hat with two-legged deer emblem and green stitched-on band. **$40-60**

Straw cowboy hat with four-legged deer emblem. **$40-60**

Over the past three decades, a bewildering array of baseball caps has been offered promoting John Deere. **Most of these can be had today for $3-15.**

Tall straw hat with multicolor band and four-legged deer logo. **$50-70**

The mesh baseball cap is arguably the most common piece of Deere headwear on the market today. **$5-10**

Stickpins

Gold John Deere corn planter stickpin. **$400-500**

John Deere Iron Clad Wagons wagon wheel pin. **$100-150**

Four-legged deer cut out stickpin. **$40-60**

Velie saddlery stickpin. **$400-500**

John Deere bronze deer over plow stickpin. **$20-40**

Velie Automobile stickpin. **$50-75**

Watches and Fobs

Ornate gold-plated oval fob with John Deere D on celluloid background, 1915-1920. **$1,400-1,600**

Ornate bronze oval fob with John Deere D on celluloid background, 1915-1920. **$600-800**

 Watch fobs were long popular premiums — at least until pocket watches were no longer commonplace.

Oval silver watch fob with raised deer over plow against red, white and blue background, 1915-1940. **$1,000-1,200**

Oval silver watch fob with raised deer over plow against cobalt blue background, 1915-1940. **$450-550**

Oval silver watch fob with raised deer over plow against turquoise background, 1915-1940. **$250-300**

Oval bronze watch fob with raised deer over plow, 1915-1940. **$900-1,000**

Watch fob with deer over plow on shield-shaped mother-of-pearl background, antlers to the rear variation. **$350-400**

Waterloo Boy watch fob with original leather strap. **$250-325**

Watch fob with deer over plow on shield-shaped mother-of-pearl background, antlers to the front variation. **$250-300**

John Deere 100th Anniversary watch fob, features John Deere bust with "He gave to the world the steel plow" legend, 1937. **$80-100**

Ornate silver cast watch fob with deer over log logo. **$100-300**

John Deere double-sided watch fob, plow on one side with "John Deere Centennial" legend. Other side has bust of John Deere. Fob attached to leather strap. **$60-100**

John Deere Velie watch fob, reads: "The name insures the quality" around perimeter. **$150-200**

John Deere walking plow watch fob. **$20-40**

Die-cast watch fob with harnessed deer inside D logo, watch fob promoting buggy and saddlery. **$200-400**

Enameled watch fob with four-legged deer logo, 1966. **$20-30**

Rectangular watch fob with four-legged deer logo, 1980s. **$30-40**

Black-faced jewel-back dress pocket watch with four-legged deer logo. **$75-150**

Rectangular watch fob with flat two-legged deer logo, 1980s. **$15-20**

White-faced jewel-back dress pocket watch with four-legged deer logo. **$75-150**

Men's digital John Deere watch, with two-legged deer and tractor logo on face. **$20-25**

CHAPTER 4
DEERE WAY OF LIFE— EMPLOYEE AND DEALER ITEMS

As memorabilia collectors get more advanced, they tend to want more uncommon items. Oftentimes they turn to dealer and factory items as a "next step." Unlike the collectibles previously discussed in this volume, all of which were intended to be widely distributed to customers or potential customers, and were produced in very large quantities (even if the number of surviving examples is low), the items in this chapter have always been relatively scarce.

A dealer may have given away thousands of matchbooks, hundreds of brochures, and dozens of caps, but most had only one or two signs. The scarcity here is obvious. Hanging on the walls of showrooms, and in service bays, was often a clock with the John Deere logo. A glance at the time was also a glance at the familiar leaping deer logo for customer and employee alike.

Factory employee identification for decades was a robust metal badge, also adorned with the leaping deer, and often surrounded by the name of the facility the employee was assigned to. Color-coding of these badges identified the employees' shift and department, and today adds color and variety to a collection of such items.

Lighted Pam clock with Quality Farm Equipment logo. **$350-450**

Canadian lighted Pam clock with Quality Farm Equipment logo. **$400-500**

Pam clock with four-legged deer logo. **$1,500-2,000**

Black, red and yellow porcelainized steel dealership sign, measuring 2 x 6 feet. **$1,500-3,000**

Lighted plastic John Deere Lawn and Garden sign with green border. **$1,000-1,500**

Lighted plastic John Deere Lawn and Garden sign with brown border. **$800-1,200**

John Deere Green Machine Authorized Parts & Service sign. **$100-1,200**

Truck door decal with Quality Farm Equipment logo. **$200-250**

John Deere Long Green Line 1965 banner. **$175-225**

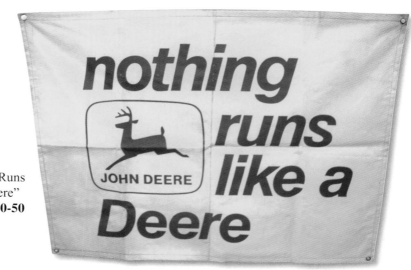

"Nothing Runs Like a Deere" banner. **$30-50**

Argentinean 730 dealer poster, including tractor illustration. **$125-175**

Argentinean 730 dealer poster, including tractor illustration. **$125-175**

John Deere dealership cardboard cutout toy display. **$175-225**

German Lanz small dealership poster. **$25-40**

1954 John Deere 127 corn picker poster. **$300-700**

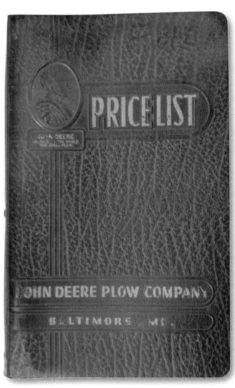

John Deere four-legged Deere promotional plaque. **$150-225**

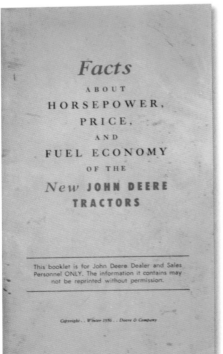

"Facts about horsepower, price and fuel economy of the new John Deere tractors" dealer salesman manual, 1956. **$30-50**

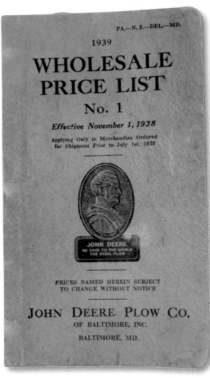

Deere published elaborate bound price lists for the use of dealership salesmen. Because of their detailed technical information, these volumes are today sought after by both memorabilia and tractor collectors. **$50-100**

Employee Badges

Deere & Webber Co., Corn Picker Plant ID badge. **$800-900**

All brass John Deere Tractor Works badge. **$300-350**

John Deere Tractor "Special" badge. **$225-275**

Foreman John Deere Tractor Works blue badge. **$250-300**

John Deere Tractor Works green badge. **$125-175**

John Deere Tractor Works black badge. **$125-175**

John Deere Tractor Works red badge. **$125-175**

Van Brunt Mfg. Co., blue badge. **$200-250**

Van Brunt Mfg. Co., black badge. **$200-250**

John Deere Plow Works black badge. **$175-225**

John Deere Harvester Works badge. **$175-225**

Factory employee identification for decades was a robust metal badge, also adorned with the leaping deer.

Union Malleable Iron Works Foreman badge. **$350-450**

John Deere Deputy Sheriff Security Badge. **$150-200**

Deere & Mansur yellow office badge. **$150-200**

All brass Deere & Mansur badge. **$300-350**

Gold John Deere Security Services Badge. **$150-200**

John Deere Security Badge. **$150-200**

John Deere Plow and Planter Works Construction Worker badge. **$75-100**

CHAPTER 5
WORKING DEERE— OWNERS AND OPERATORS ITEMS

Arguably the collectibles most in demand among those in this book are the items relating to the owning and operating of John Deere equipment. The operator's manual for a Model D is just as applicable today as it was in 1937. The vintage tractor buff is likely to have more than one copy—a well-worn original (or reprint) in the shop where he maintains his collection, and a pristine original "for show." Demand at swap meets for such items is substantial, with competition between literature collectors and tractor restorers. Although some of these documents can be rather pricey in their own right, even at $200, a manual rarely represents one percent of the cost of restoration of a tractor or implement.

Similarly, collectors appreciate the vintage logos found on certain service parts and their packaging. Yet the parts themselves in many instances are also in demand from those who are restoring their vintage machine.

Operator's Repair and Parts Manuals

Overtime tractor
instruction book.
$175-200

John Deere G instruction book. **$50-60**

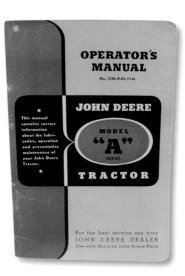

John Deere Model A operator's manual. **$30-40**

John Deere Gold Medal cream separator operator's manual. **$75-85**

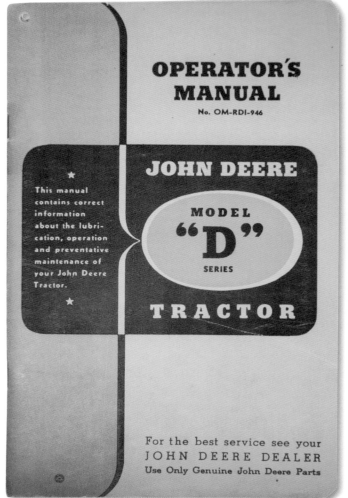

John Deere D operator's manual. **$50-60**

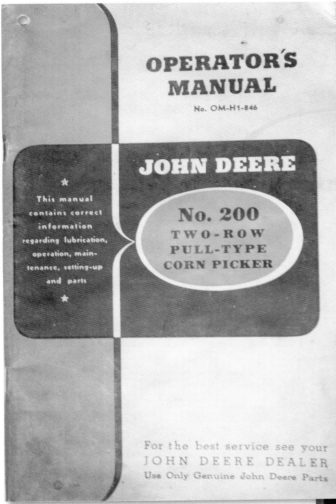

John Deere 200 corn picker operator's manual. **$20-25**

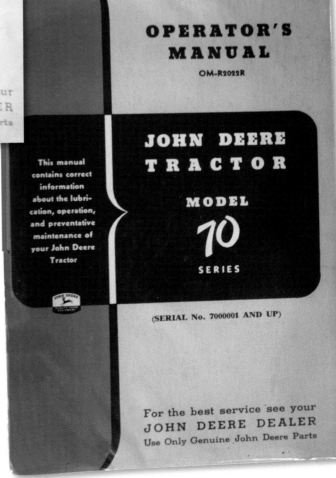

John Deere 70 gas operator's manual. **$60-70**

John Deere 70
diesel operator's
manual. **$60-70**

John Deere 730
diesel operator's
manual. **$15-25**

OPERATOR'S MANUAL
OM-R2088R

JOHN DEERE
820
DIESEL TRACTOR
WITH V-4 GASOLINE CRANKING ENGINE
(Serial No. 8203100-   )

John Deere 820 diesel operator's manual. **$15-25**

Various editions of the operator's manuals were published through the years, as can be seen by these 1010 operator's manuals. **$15-25 each**

OPERATOR'S MANUAL
OM-T16142T

JOHN DEERE
1010 SERIES
TRACTORS
(Serial No. 31001-Up)

JOHN DEERE
1010 ROW-CROP
UTILITY
GASOLINE
TRACTOR

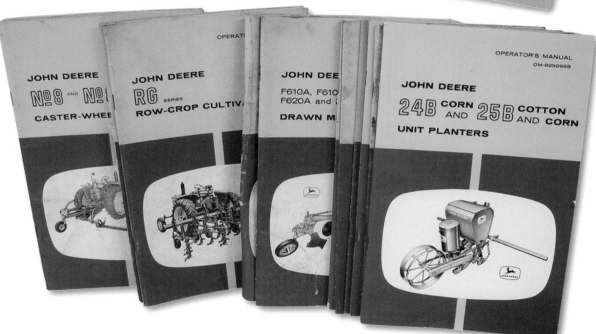

Typically, implement and accessory manuals such as these are less sought after—hence less valuable—than the manuals for the tractors themselves, although the implement manuals tend to be harder to find. **$5-15**

JOHN DEERE TRACTOR COMPANY

REPAIR CATALOG
No. 50-R

FOR

JOHN DEERE
GENERAL PURPOSE, WIDE
TREAD AND ORCHARD
TRACTORS

EFFECTIVE APRIL 15, 1940

JOHN DEERE TRACTOR CO.
WATERLOO, IOWA, U. S. A.

SUPERSEDES ALL PREVIOUS EDITIONS

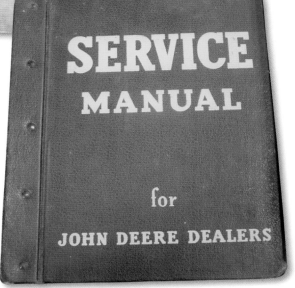

Repair and parts manuals range from simple softbound documents of only a few pages to massive books in hard binders. Most are found heavily soiled from use in shops or on parts counters, and pristine examples command a substantial premium. Prices very widely, dependant largely on the popularity—and demand—of the tractor or implement covered. **$25-400**

Service Parts and Tools

Box of 50 husking pegs. **$30-50**

AR28610 filter element. **$20-25**

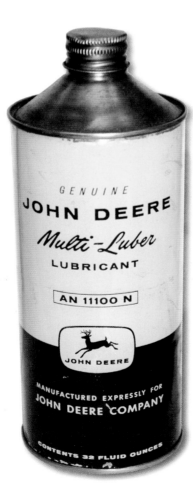

Can of John Deere multi-luber lubricant with four-legged deer logo. **$20-40**

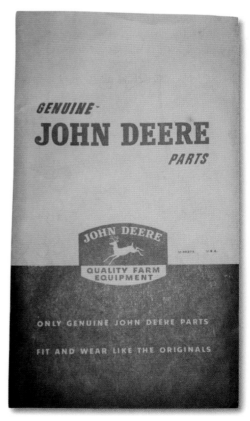

Paper parts sack with Quality Farm Equipment logo. **$15-20**

John Deere sugar cane mill wrench made by Crescent. **$600-800**

Paper parts sack with four-legged deer logo. **$15-20**

Starting, lighting and ignition parts assortment in plastic tray with four-legged deer logo. **$300-500**

Cut out Deere steel toolbox that mounted on implement drawbar. **$100-150**

Collectors appreciate the vintage logos found on certain parts and their packaging.

CHAPTER 6

VINTAGE DEERE— MISCELLANEOUS COLLECTIBLES FROM YEARS GONE BY

With a history spanning almost 200 years, it should not be a surprise that some items have been produced that carry the John Deere name, but don't fit neatly into any of the previous categories. Some are branch house items that could have been listed in the Way of Life chapter, others are packaging that with some stretching could have been included in Chapter 5—yet such categorization wouldn't have really fit.

Some of these are extremely rare, and may represent the life goal of some collectors, others are rather common, but interesting. As a whole, they represent the breadth of Deere's efforts through the years, and the firm's proud history.

Plaster busts of John Deere were issued to branch houses during the company's 1937 centennial celebration. Only a handful of these busts, which were copied from the original bronze at Deere's headquarters, were made. **$30,000-40,000**

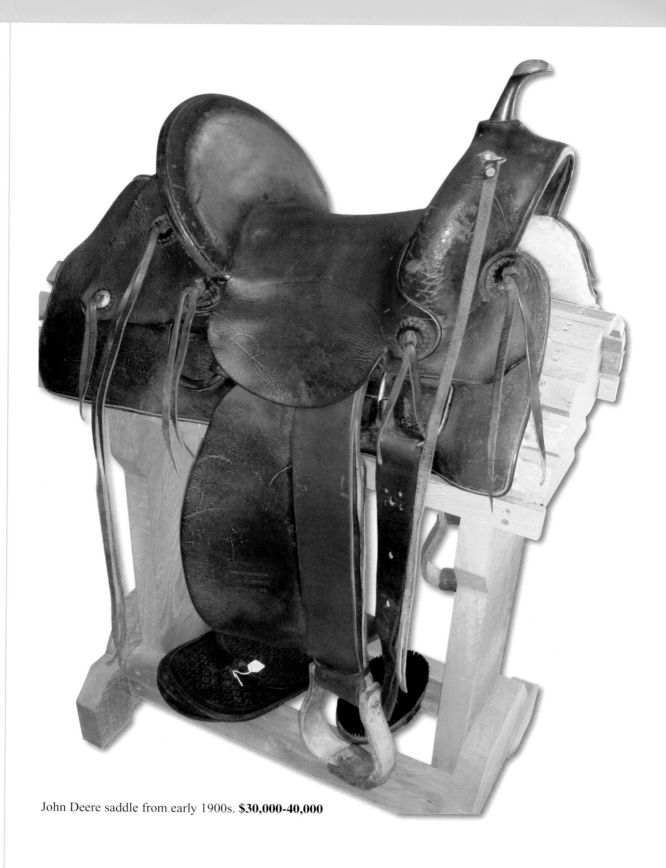

John Deere saddle from early 1900s. **$30,000-40,000**

John Deere buggy chromolithograph with logo in corner, in original frame. **$3,000-3,750**

 Some of these items are extremely rare, and may represent the life goal of some collectors.

Chromolithograph of deer standing on hill overlooking Deere factory, in original frame. **$2,000-3,000**

This plow on plaque presentation item was probably issued during the John Deere centennial. **$800-1,000**

Argentinean sales award consisting of a miniature plow mounted on a plaque. **$400-500**

REPLICA DEL PRIMER ARADO
DE ACERO CONSTRUIDO POR
JOHN DEERE EN GRAND DETOUR
ILLINOIS U.S.A. - 1837

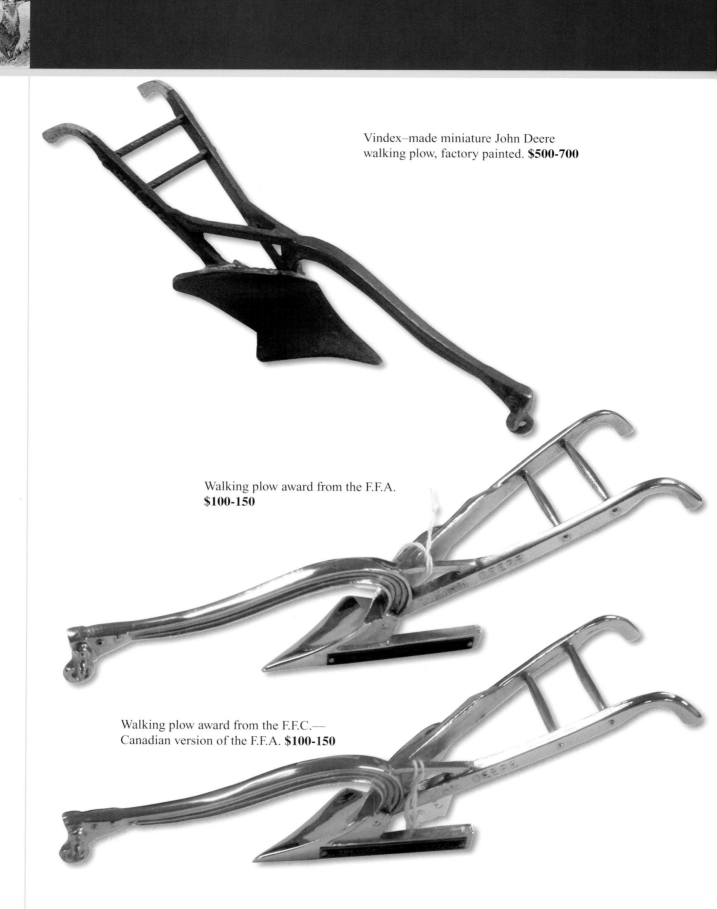

Vindex–made miniature John Deere walking plow, factory painted. **$500-700**

Walking plow award from the F.F.A. **$100-150**

Walking plow award from the F.F.C.— Canadian version of the F.F.A. **$100-150**

Walking plow award from the N.F.A.—
Negro version of the F.F.A. **$400-500**

John Deere Centennial cigar band. **$200-250**

This walnut writing desk was produced
for John Deere's 150th anniversary,
and includes an inset 150th anniversary
medallion. **$400-450**

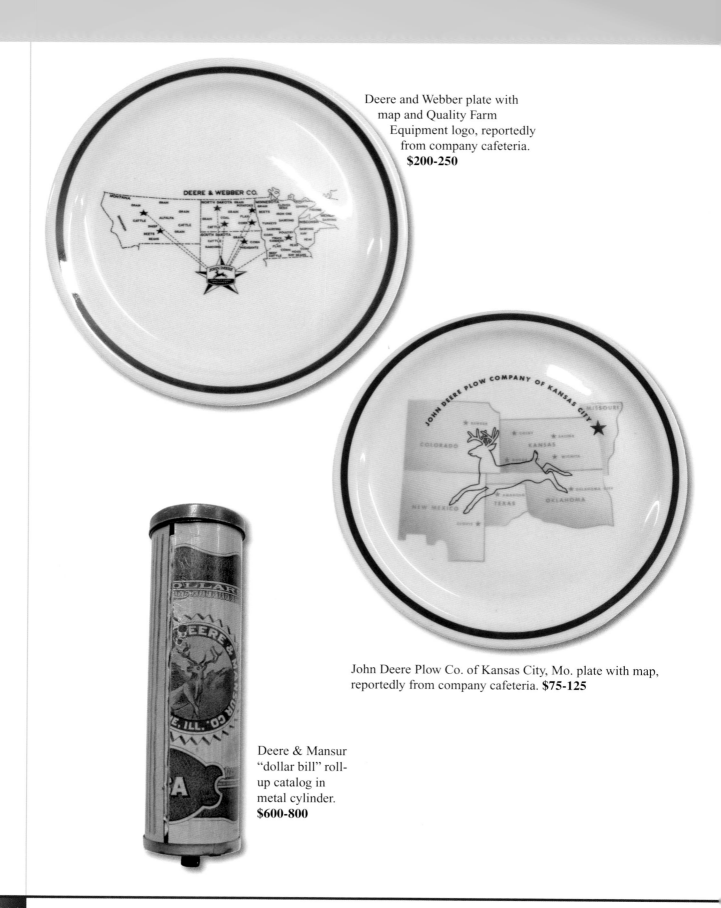

Deere and Webber plate with map and Quality Farm Equipment logo, reportedly from company cafeteria. **$200-250**

John Deere Plow Co. of Kansas City, Mo. plate with map, reportedly from company cafeteria. **$75-125**

Deere & Mansur "dollar bill" roll-up catalog in metal cylinder. **$600-800**

John Deere Centennial medallion set consisting of two eight-inch diameter "coins." **$2,500-3,500**

Coin with John Deere's birth and death dates. **$30-60**

Cast iron letter holder with original paint—**beware of reproductions**. **$1,500-1,700**

Empty Vitrea John Deere Fertilizer plastic bag. **$400-600**

John Deere Fertilizer soil sample bag. **$350-550**

John Deere 45 Fertilizer
paper bag. **$400-500**

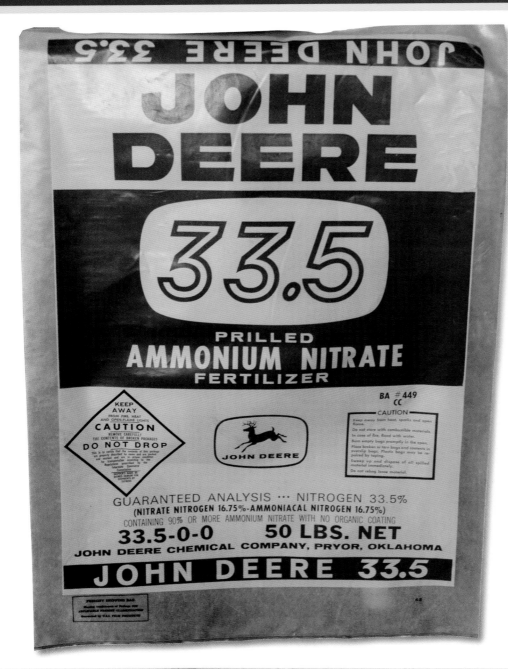

John Deere 33.5 Fertilizer plastic bag. **$300-400**

Tractor Works employee bumper sticker with 1968-1999 leaping deer logo. **$25-50**

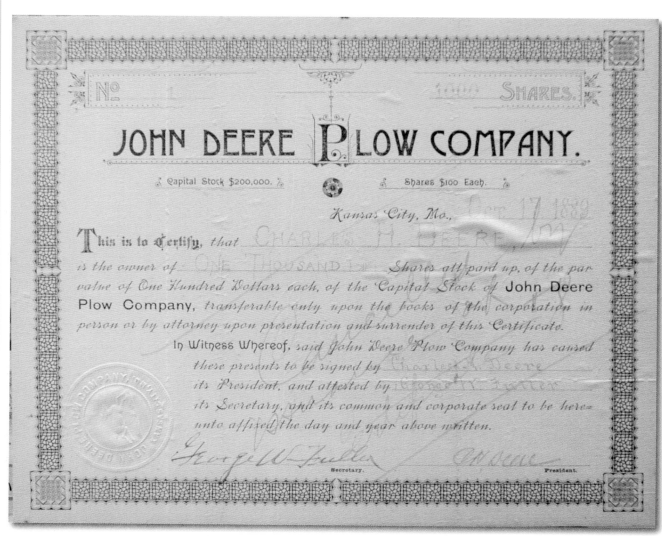

John Deere Plow Co. stock certificate. **$1,500-2,000**

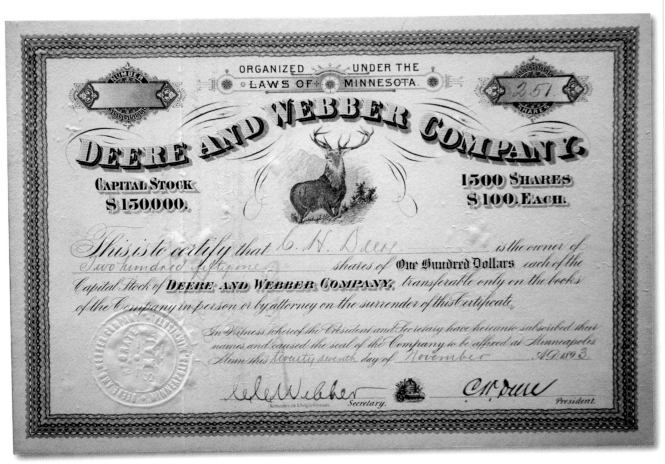

Deere and Webber Co. stock certificate. **$1,500-2,000**

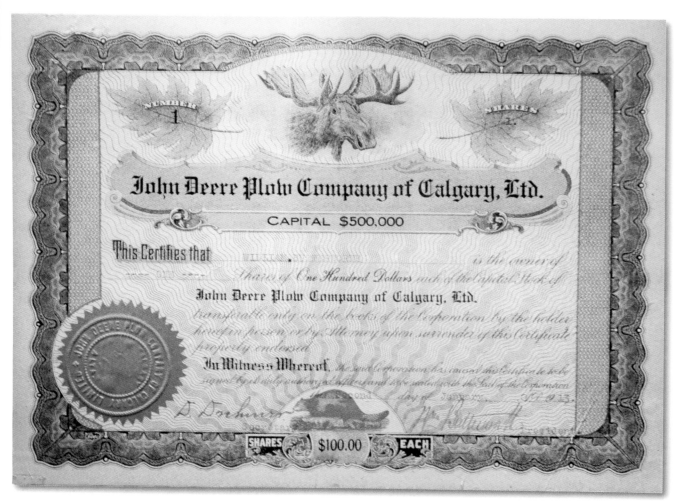

John Deere Plow Co. of Calgary stock certificate. **$1,000-1,500**

John Deere
Plow Co. of San
Francisco stock
certificate.
$800-1,200

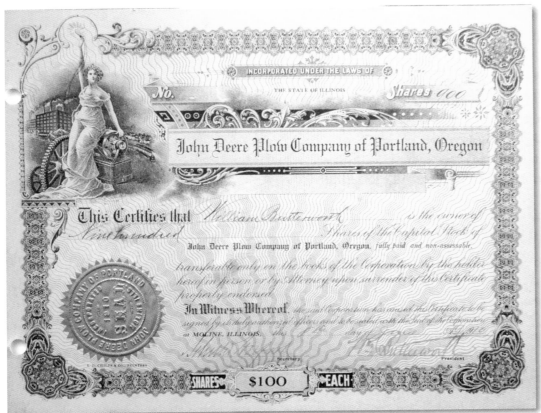

John Deere Plow
Co. of Portland,
Ore. stock
certificate.
$800-1,200

CHAPTER 7
MINIATURE DEERE— TOYS AND MODELS

One of the most popular collecting niches of John Deere memorabilia is the numerous toys and models created through the years. Like so many of the items in this book, these were not originally targeted at "collectors," but rather were simply toys. "Junior farmers" wanted to play with miniature replicas of the equipment they saw in daily use on their dad's or granddad's farm. Indeed, for generations, John Deere dealers were the most common outlets for these toys.

Ertl is a name permanently linked to John Deere toys. Fred Ertl Sr. produced his first toy John Deere tractor in the basement of the family's Dubuque, Iowa home in late 1945. That first tractor was a 1/16-scale replica of the John Deere Model A—and that scale has remained popular since.

As time passed other names became associated with Deere toys: Carter Tru-Scale, Eska Co., SpecCast, Scale Models, and a range of other makers who entered the arena. The products these companies produced evolved over time as well, transitioning from rugged toys for children to realistic models marketed to adults.

Collecting both vintage and current die-cast is today a hobby unto its own. As such, there are a number of specialized periodicals and books, such as the "Standard Catalog of® Farm Toys" that provide comprehensive listings of these toys and models. If toys and models are your primary interest, such publications would be a wise investment.

However, it is rare indeed to find a John Deere collector without at least a few toys or models in his or her collection, and toys frequently surface at farm auctions. Hence, a representative sampling of such items is included here. As with any of the collectibles listed in this book, condition is the key to value, and to obtain top prices, the toys must be unused and in their original box. Beware, however, that reproduction parts and decals have been produced, and repaired and restored tractors are worth far less than excellent condition originals.

The listings are arranged first in descending order by scale, and then by prototype tractor or implement model number. That is, a 1/16- scale Model R will be found before a 1/64-scale Model A. The toy manufacturer's stock number is included wherever possible, as well as the date of initial release. Beware that multiple replicas of a given model tractor have been produced on many occasions, making positive identification important.

Photo courtesy of Doug Mitchell.

Pedal Tractors

John Deere A pedal tractor sold by Eska. Made in the 1950s. **$4,000-5,000**

John Deere 10 pedal tractor sold by Eska, with four holes between block and hood. Made in the 1960s. **$500-900**

John Deere 10 Pedal tractor sold by Eska, with three holes between block and hood. Made in the 1960s. **$475-850**

John Deere 20 pedal tractor sold by Eska. Made in the mid-to-late 1960s. **$200-700**

John Deere 30 pedal tractor made by Ertl. Cast into right side of tractor near pedal is "Model NO. 520," made from 1973 through 1978. The later 40 and 50 used the same casting (with the same number cast in place), but with different decals. **$150-500**

John Deere 55 pedal tractor made by Ertl. Cast into right side of tractor near pedal is "Stock NO. 520." **$500-1,500**

John Deere 130 Pedal tractor sold by Eska, with two holes between upper part of block and hood. Made in the 1970s. Casting number "531." **$600-1,100**

John Deere 60 pedal tractor sold by Eska, small version. Made in the 1950s. **$500-900**

John Deere 60 pedal tractor sold by Eska, large version. Made in the 1950s. **$500-900**

John Deere 620 pedal tractor sold by Eska. Made in the 1950s. **$600-1,000**

1/16 Scale

Model A, 1947, Ertl. **$75-400**

Photo courtesy of Doug Mitchell.

1934 Model A, 1985, Ertl, stock number "539DO." **$10-20**

Model A With Man, 2003, Ertl, stock number "15571." **$10-20**

Photo courtesy of Doug Mitchell.

Styled A, 2000, Ertl, stock number "15071." **$15-20**

Photo courtesy of Doug Mitchell.

Photo courtesy of Doug Mitchell.

Styled Model A, with man, gold plated, 2003, Ertl stock number "15569A." **$25-70**

Photo courtesy of Doug Mitchell.

Model A with 290 Cultivator, Ertl Precision Classics Special Edition "2," 1992, stock number "5633." **$200-400**

1949 Model AR, 1993, Ertl, stock number "5680." **$30-60**

 It is rare indeed to find a John Deere collector without at least a few toys or models in his or her collection.

Photo courtesy of Doug Mitchell.

Model AW with Umbrella, 2000, Ertl, stock number "15070A." **$40-50**

Photo courtesy of Doug Mitchell.

Styled Model B, 1997, Ertl Precision Classics Special Edition "12," stock number "5107." **$125-200**

Model B, 1994, Collector Classics Scale Models, stock number "FB2352." **$50-60**

Photo courtesy of Doug Mitchell.

1935 Model BR, Ertl, stock number "5586." **$20-35**

Photo courtesy of Doug Mitchell.

Photos courtesy of Doug Mitchell.

Model BW, 2003, Ertl, stock number "15348." **$15-30**

Model BW, John Deere's 200th Birthday edition, with umbrella, 2004, Ertl, stock number "15645A." **$15-35**

Photo courtesy of Doug Mitchell.

1923 Model D, Ertl, stock number "500." **$10-25**

Photo courtesy of Doug Mitchell.

1953 Model D, 1990, Ertl, stock number "5596." **$20-30**

Model D, 1994, Ertl, stock number "5596." **$35-65**

Photo courtesy of Doug Mitchell.

Model D, 75th Anniversary, 1999, Ertl, stock number "5198DA." **$20-50**

Photo courtesy of Doug Mitchell.

1937 Model G, 1991, Ertl, stock number "548." **$15-25**

Photo courtesy of Doug Mitchell.

Model G Wide Front, 1997, Ertl, stock number "5103DA." **$20-40**

1928 Model GP, 1994, Ertl, stock number "5801." **$10-30**

Photo courtesy of Doug Mitchell.

1930 Model GP Wide Tread, steel wheels, 1995, Ertl, stock number "5787." **$15-30**

Model H, 2000, Ertl,
stock number "15034."
$25-35

Photos courtesy of Doug Mitchell.

Photo courtesy of Doug Mitchell.

Model L, 2004, SpecCast, stock number "JDM176." **$25-35**

Photo courtesy of Doug Mitchell.

Lindeman crawler with cultivator, 2006, SpecCast, stock number "JDM 190." **$35-45**

Model M with Two Bottom Plow, 2006, SpecCast, stock number "JDM 200." **$50-70**

Photo courtesy of Doug Mitchell.

Model M, 1986, Ertl, stock number "540." **$10-15**

Photo courtesy of Doug Mitchell.

Photo courtesy of Doug Mitchell.

Model MC Crawler, 1996, SpecCast, stock number "JDM096." **$15-45**

Photos courtesy of Doug Mitchell.

1949 Model MT, 1996, SpecCast, stock number "JDM-073." **$50-60**

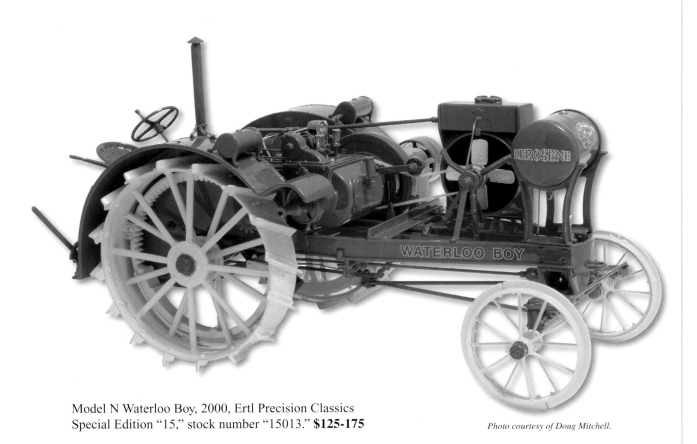

Model N Waterloo Boy, 2000, Ertl Precision Classics
Special Edition "15," stock number "15013." **$125-175**

Photo courtesy of Doug Mitchell.

Model "P" General Purpose, narrow front, steel wheels, with umbrella, 75th Anniversary Edition, 2005, Ertl, stock number "15742A." **$25-35**

Photo courtesy of Doug Mitchell.

Model R 1915 Waterloo Boy, 1988, Ertl, stock number "559." **$10-15**

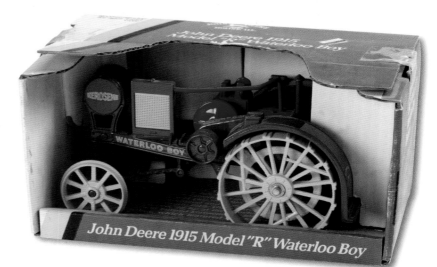

Photos courtesy of Doug Mitchell.

Model R, 1985, Ertl, stock number "544." **$20-30**

Utility Tractor, 1983, Ertl, stock number "501." **$10-20**

Photo courtesy of Doug Mitchell.

John Deere 40 Crawler with blade, green and yellow, Esca/Carter, 1954, rubber tracks. **$150-600**

John Deere Model 40 Crawler with blade, industrial yellow, Esca/Carter, 1954, rubber tracks. **$200-750**

John Deere Model 40 Crawler, Ertl, 1998, rubber tracks, stock number "5072." **$25-40**

Photo courtesy of Doug Mitchell.

Model 60, 2002, Ertl, stock number "15189." **$10-20**

Photos courtesy of Doug Mitchell.

 Beware that reproduction parts and decals have been produced, and repaired and restored tractors are worth far less than excellent condition originals.

Model 60 with Picker/Sheller, 2007, Ertl, stock number "15816." **$35-65**

Photo courtesy of Doug Mitchell.

Photo courtesy of Doug Mitchell.

1953 Model 60 Orchard, 1993, Ertl, stock number "5679." **$15-25**

Photo courtesy of Doug Mitchell.

1953 Model 70, 1991, Ertl, stock number "5611." **$10-25**

Model 140 Lawn and Garden tractor with trailer, 1974, Ertl. **$60-275**

Photo courtesy of Doug Mitchell.

Model 420 crawler with dozer blade, 1960s Eska. **$150-550**

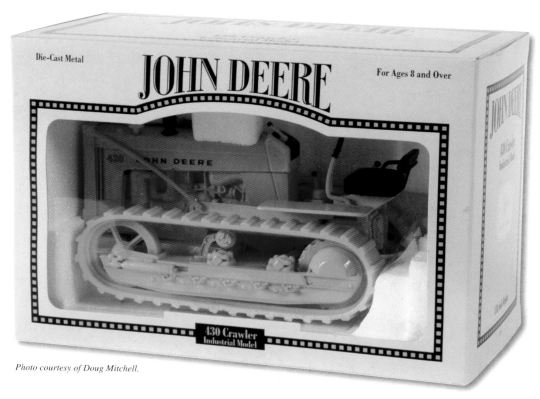

Photo courtesy of Doug Mitchell.

Model 430 Crawler, 1997, Ertl, stock number "5771." **$10-25**

Model 440 Crawler, 2005, Ertl,
stock number "15760." **$20-25**

Photo courtesy of Doug Mitchell.

Model 440 Industrial,
1950s, Ertl. **$250-1,000**

Model 520, 2002, Ertl,
stock number "15360."
$10-25

Photo courtesy of Doug Mitchell.

Model 620, 1950s, Carter/Esca. **$150-1,000**

Model 620, 2002, Ertl, stock number "15428." **$10-25**

Photo courtesy of Doug Mitchell.

Photo courtesy of Doug Mitchell.

Model 620 Orchard, 1992, Ertl, Expo 3, stock number "5678DA." **$30-40**

Photo courtesy of Doug Mitchell.

1958 Model 630 LP, 1989, Ertl, stock number "5590." **$20-40**

Photo courtesy of Doug Mitchell.

Model 720 and 820 50th Anniversary Set, 2006, Ertl, stock number "15795A." **$60-80**

Photo courtesy of Doug Mitchell.

Model 720 with 80 Blade and 45 Loader, 2000, Ertl, Precision Classics Special Edition "18," stock number "15165." **$150-200**

1956 Model 820, 1993, Ertl, stock number "5705." **$30-40**

Photo courtesy of Doug Mitchell.

Model 830, 2004, Ertl, stock number "15592." **$30-35**

Photo courtesy of Doug Mitchell.

Model 1010, 2001, Ertl, stock number "15191." **$10-20**

1960 Model 3010, 1992, Ertl, stock number "5635." **$20-35**

Photos courtesy of Doug Mitchell.

Model 3010 Factory Error, 1/2 gas motor, 1/2 diesel, 1992, Ertl, stock number "5635." **$25-45**

1960-1964 Model 3010, Ertl, Precision Classics Special Edition "20," 2001, stock number "15210." **$125-175**

Photo courtesy of Doug Mitchell.

1961 Model 4010 Diesel, 1994, Ertl, stock number "5716DO." **$40-60**

Photo courtesy of Doug Mitchell.

COLLECTOR'S EDITION 1961 "4010" Tractor

1961 Model 4010, Collectors Edition, 1994, Ertl, stock number "5716DA." **$30-60**

Photo courtesy of Doug Mitchell.

Model 4020 tractor with 237 Corn Picker, Ertl, Precision Classics Special Edition "14," 2001, stock number "5083." **$150-200**

Photo courtesy of Doug Mitchell.

Model 4440 with duals, 1979, Ertl, stock number "542." **$30-90**

Model 4440 with weights, radio control, Ertl, stock number "31." **$25-75**

Photo courtesy of Doug Mitchell.

Photo courtesy of Doug Mitchell.

Model 4455 MFWD, 1992, Ertl, stock number "5584." **$40-50**

Photo courtesy of Doug Mitchell.

Model 4955 MFWD with duals and weights, 1989, Ertl, stock number "5587." **$25-60**

Model 6400 Row Crop, Ertl, 1993, stock number "5666." **$20-30**

Photo courtesy of Doug Mitchell.

Model 7520 Four-Wheel Drive, with air cleaner, 1972, Ertl, stock number "510." **$200-600**

Model 8760 Four-Wheel Drive, 1992, Ertl, stock number "5715." **$50-75**

Model 6600 combine with grain head, chain drive and metal reel, Ertl. **$100-400**

KBA Disc Harrow, 1950 Eska. **$100-250**

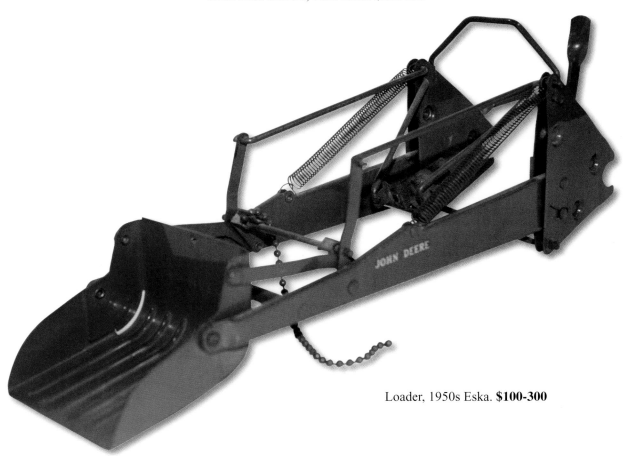

Loader, 1950s Eska. **$100-300**

Mower Conditioner, 1977, Ertl, stock number "596." **$15-35**

1/25 Scale

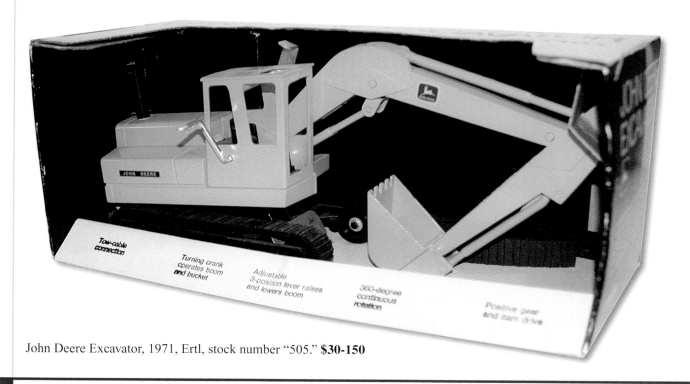

John Deere Excavator, 1971, Ertl, stock number "505." **$30-150**

1/28 Scale

Photo courtesy of Doug Mitchell.

1938 28 x 46 Thresher, 1994, SpecCast, stock number "JDM-040." **$50-65**

1/32 Scale

Photo courtesy of Doug Mitchell.

Overtime Tractor, 1990, Ertl, stock number "5811." **$10-15**

550G Crawler, 1996, Ertl, stock number "5673." **$10-20**

Skid Steer Loader 6675, 1994, Ertl, stock number "5790." **$7-15**

1/38 Scale

1926 Mack Bulldog delivery van coin bank lettered "John Deere No. 101." Mack truck, 1984, Ertl, stock number "0531." **$20-30**

1/43 Scale

1934 Model A, 1992, Ertl, stock number "5598." **$5-10**

Photo courtesy of Doug Mitchell.

1/64 Scale

"Innovations in John Deere Tractor Design" in Deere cardboard tray. **$150-225**

Model 830, 2005, Ertl. **$8-15**

Photo courtesy of Doug Mitchell.

Model 8850, 1983, Ertl, stock number "575." **$8-15**

Photo courtesy of Doug Mitchell.

Photo courtesy of Doug Mitchell.

Model 9400, Ertl, stock number "5937." **$8-15**

Model A with Farmer, 1995, Ertl. **$15-25**

Photo courtesy of Doug Mitchell.

Model B. **$5-10**

Photo courtesy of Doug Mitchell.

Miscellaneous

Original Buddy Lee John Deere doll. **$900-1,100**

Photo courtesy of Doug Mitchell.

"Little Johnny Dearest" stuffed green
and yellow deer, 1980s. **$20-30**

CHAPTER 8
MODERN COLLECTIBLES —HOME AND GARDEN ITEMS

Starting in the late 1980s, John Deere began to "cash in" on the brand recognition. An increasing number of apparel appeared, and by the dawn of the 21st century, the John Deere name appeared on a bewildering array of licensed products.

Whereas the items discussed in previous chapters were produced in the normal course of business to be simply what they were—be that a service manual, sales brochure or advertising matchbook, and later evolved into a collectible— that is not the case for the items shown in this chapter. These items have been produced specifically for marketing to those who want to decorate the home in a John Deere or farm theme, or to be sold to John Deere collectors.

The items are attractive, colorful and neat, and some indeed may become truly collectible. However, in this and all other hobbies, as a rule, if an item comes in a package marked "collectible"—it probably isn't! By all means purchase and enjoy these items for what they are, but don't expect your heirs to use these to fund their college education.

One-foot-tall John Deere oil lantern with glass globe. **$15-25**

John Deere ceiling fan light pull made by Key Enterprises Inc., features 2 x 2-inch tractor. **$3-7**

Nightlight featuring stained glass John Deere tractor. **$10-15**

John Deere suspenders, still in original package, Embroidery Plus. **$10-15**

Towel made by Canon with John Deere name and tractor. **$10-20**

Wind chime, 36 x 6-1/2-inch, with John Deere 720, maker unknown. **$30-40**

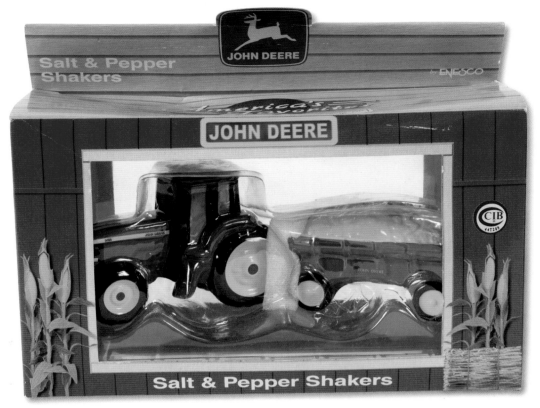

Salt and Pepper Shakers, made by Enesco in 1998, resembling 8400 tractor and wagon. **$4-8**

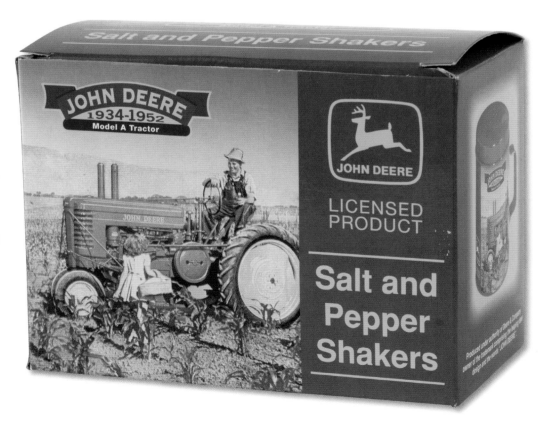

Tin salt and pepper shakers, decorated with John Deere Model A tractor, made in 2000. **$3-5**

John Deere Lawn and Garden tractor salt and pepper shakers made in 1999 by Enesco. Driver is one piece; tractor is the other. **$10-20**

Set of six John Deere coasters, with tin container. **$8-12**

Set of four solid cork 3-3/4 x 3-3/4-inch coasters printed with two scenes. One a 1934-1952 Model A tractor, the other a 1939-1947 Model H. Stock number "D811." **$3-8**

John Deere Snow Globe, "The Farmer in the Dell" musical when wound, Enesco, shows farmer on tractor. **$25-35**

John Deere Model A ceramic Christmas ornament, made by Enesco in 2000, box reads "Hanging Ornament." **$5-10**

John Deere 7410 ceramic Christmas ornament by Enesco. **$3-5**

1996 Christmas ornament made by SpecCast featuring "John Deere's Home Grand Detour, IL." Made of pewter, the circular ornament came in cloth bag. **$20-25**

John Deere Christmas ornament featuring cow on tractor with tree in loader. Part of Mary's Moo Moos line made by Enesco in 2001. **$15-20**

Cow standing by tractor, statue of the month December, by Mary's Moo Moos. **$10-15**

Metal tray made in 2002 decorated with John Deere Model A. **$5-10**

John Deere snack set, with round tray or bowl, measuring 9-1/4 inches across, and mug measuring 4-1/4 inches tall. **$7-10**

John Deere mug, marketed by Gibson, "Nothing Runs Like a Deere," yellow squares on white mug. **$2-3**

Pair of mugs with styled Model A on each. **$2-3**

Soup mug, white, by Gifts etc., with tractor and "Nothing Runs Like a Deere." **$1-3**

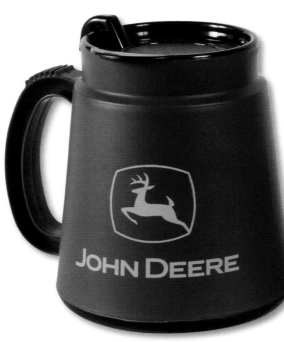

Insulated 20-ounce travel mugs by Betras. **$4-8 each**

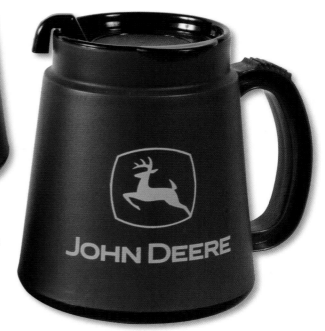

Green John Deere mug by Gibson with "John Deere Moline, IL" markings. **$2-3**

Wall-mount John Deere bottle opener, made by Starr, Brown Mfg. Co., Atlanta, Ga., 2001. **$5-10**

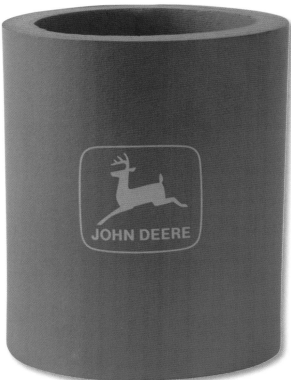

John Deere can koozie, green with two-legged deer logo.
$2-3

"Days of Splendor" plate from Danbury Mint by artist Mort Kunstler. Eight-inch diameter plate with gold rim. Stock number "#E2864." **$10-15**

"Golden Harvest" plate from Danbury Mint by artist Mort Kunstler. Eight-inch diameter plate with gold rim. Stock number "#E2864." **$10-15**

Blanket, yellow on one side, green on the other. **$15-20**

Flag with John Deere Model B tractor. **$10-20**

John Deere birdhouse, green with yellow roof. **$5-15**

License plate decorated with legend "Nothing Runs Like a Deere." **$4-8**

"John Deere Parking Only" license plate with four-legged deer logo. **$5-10**

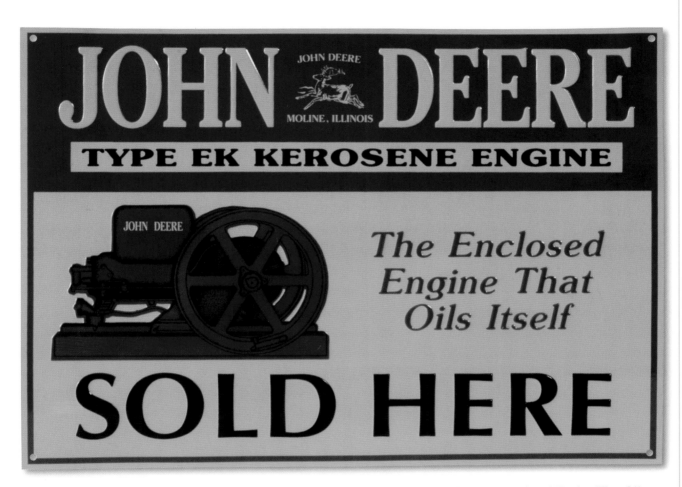

John Deere sign, yellow and green, rectangle "John Deere Type EK Kerosene Engine, The Enclosed Engine That Oils Itself, SOLD HERE." **$8-12**

Porcelain enameled advertising manufactured by Ande Rooney firm which features the "V is for Victory John Deere" 1945 calendar artwork of a woman driving tractor waving to troops. **$8-15**

Green and yellow "John Deere Collector" sign with 730 and D model tractors on it. **$5-10**

Green plastic indoor/outdoor thermometer depicting farm scene. The circular thermometer has scales reading in both Celsius and Fahrenheit. **$8-15**

John Deere trading cards with tractor photos, set of 60 cards. **$5-10**

John Deere tin mini lunch box, made by The Tin Box Co. Features two latches, yellow plastic handle, four-legged deer logo and a tractor on it. **$8-12**

7610 tractor nightlight, made of plastic in China. **$8-12**

Embroidered cloth patch with two-legged deer logo. **$5-10**

John Deere steering wheel spinner knob, "John Deere Quality Farm Equipment" logo. **$8-15**

Trailer hitch ball cover. **$5-10**

Four-inch ceramic clock with John Deere tractor. **$10-20**

Resin John Deere 2 x 3-inch picture frame. **$2-3**

FROM THE SHED TO THE SHELF

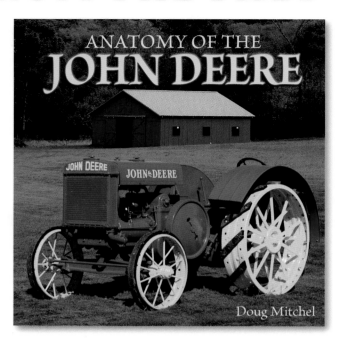

Anatomy of the John Deere

by Doug Mitchel

Feed your interest in the king of the fields with this lavishly illustrated John Deere book, covering 40+tractors - featured in 300+ color photos along with historical and performance details.

Softcover • 10-3/4 x 10-3/4 • 256 pages
300+ color photos
Item# Z0982 • $35.00

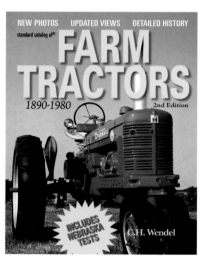

**Standard Catalog of® Farm Tractors
1890-1980**
2nd Edition
by C. H. Wendel
Gauge the true performance of farm tractors manufactured from 1890-1980 with this detail rich guide. Plus, review Nebraska Tractor Test data for most models.
Softcover • 8-½ x 11 • 752 pages
1,800+ b&w photos

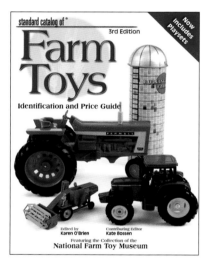

Standard Catalog of® Farm Toys
Identification and Price Guide
3rd Edition
by Karen O'Brien
Cultivate the exact farm toy collection you desire by accessing historical details, detailed descriptions and secondary market prices for 1:8 to 1:64 scale farm toys, dating back to the 1920s.
Softcover • 8-1/4 x 10-7/8 • 496 pages
5,000+ b&w photos • 96 color photos
Item# Z0993 • $29.99

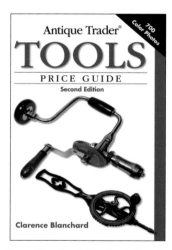

Antique Trader® Tools Price Guide
2nd Edition
by Clarence Blanchard
Discover the value of ingenious antique tools that helped beautify and build the nation. This full-color guide covers antique hand tools including planes and saws, levels and axes, and much more.
Softcover • 6 x 9 • 304 pages
700+ color photos
Item# Z0841 • $22.99

Order directly from the publisher at **www.krausebooks.com**

Krause Publications, Offer **ACB8**
P.O. Box 5009
Iola, WI 54945-5009
www.krausebooks.com

Call 800-258-0929 8 a.m. - 5 p.m. to order direct from the publisher, or vis booksellers nationwide or antiques and hobby shops.

Please reference offer **ACB8** with all direct-to-publisher orders

Get News to Use at www.antiquetrader.com